SUGAR
FLOWERS

VOLUME 2

Jacqueline Butler

DAVID & CHARLES

www.davidandcharles.com

Contents

INTRODUCTION

Ever since learning how to bake at a young age I've been in love with cake! I also love delicate, meticulous details and flowers, so it's not a surprise I ended up building a business in wedding cake design. Petalsweet was formed after my own journey studying cake decorating and sugar flowers and has been followed with years of practice to create my own modern, stylized aesthetic.

Writing my first book, *Modern Sugar Flowers*, was an amazing opportunity to share some of my favorite processes for making beautiful sugar flowers that are both achievable and profitable within a cake business. Thank you so much to all of you who purchased the book, and for sharing your beautiful flowers and cakes!

Thoughts about writing volume two began with the few flowers that didn't make it into the first book, and from there it didn't take long to put together a new list of flowers I was excited to share. So, here you'll find my favorite new flowers and my most trusted staples broken down into simple, easy-to-follow steps. And a small spotlight on greenery and berries, which can be used to give arrangements a more relaxed, organic feel. The cake projects are a fun mix of little cakes and single tiers, and a few more elaborate designs that I hope will inspire you to try something new.

My simple, signature and fool-proof *formula* for putting flowers together is still the same. Begin with a pretty base of green and white, and then add some pastels to complete the look. It's easy to do, and always looks fresh. I've expanded my color palette a bit to include a few deeper colors and I hope you enjoy the additions.

I hope this book not only teaches you the tips and techniques to achieve new sugar flowers, but also gives you the confidence to create something beautiful for your clients or to share with loved ones. Enjoy the process, and happy flower making!

Jacqueline x

TOOLS & SUPPLIES

ESSENTIAL TOOL KIT

Each flower lesson begins with a list of the specific supplies you will need. Please read through all of the instructions before you start, to make sure you have all of the necessary tools.

1 Groove board: a non-stick sugarcraft rolling board with grooves for making wired leaves and flowers

2 Petal protector or acetate sheet to keep rolled paste and cut petals from drying too quickly

3 Needle tool

4 JEM veining tool

5 Mini palette knife

6 Tweezers

7 Set of sugarcraft modeling tools

8 Mini Celpin

9 Celpin

10 Knife/scribing tool

11 Dresden tool

12 Metal ball tools in variety of sizes

13 Foam petal pad

14 Small straight embroidery scissors

15 Sharp scissors

16 Toothpick (cocktail stick)

17 Wooden skewer

18 Small non-stick rolling pin

19 Mini rolling pin

20 Wire cutters

21 Pliers, for making hooks in wires, and to aid in flower arranging

22 Vegetable shortening (white vegetable fat)

23 Sugar glue and a small brush

24 Cornstarch (cornflour)

25 Detail paintbrush

26 Flat and round paintbrushes for dusting and detailed work

SPECIALIZED TOOLS AND SUPPLIES

1 Styrofoam balls in a variety of sizes

2 Petal dust

3 Gel food colors

4 Silicone leaf veiners

5 Metal petal cutter (petunia)

6 Plastic half sphere molds

7 Hanging rack

8 Acoustic "bumpy" foam for drying petals and leaves

9 Silicone petal veiners

10 Cotton sewing thread

11 Styrofoam buds (CelBuds)

12 "Pollen" created with unflavored gelatin mixed with petal dust (see Getting Started)

13 Floral tape

14 Silcone leaf veiners (all-purpose)

15 Metal petal cutters (small rose petals)

16 Metal petal cutters (multi-use for petals and leaves)

17 Stamens

18 Florist wire

19 Waxed dental floss

Getting Started

I've gathered the essential information and techniques that I use in my flower making and put them all together in this chapter. You can refer back to this section whenever you need a refresher, or if you are trying a technique for the first time.

(1)

tip

When using cornstarch (cornflour) and shortening, use very small amounts to prevent the paste from drying out or becoming greasy and separating.

(2)

USING GUMPASTE

A soft, pliable sugar dough made with an added gum agent, gumpaste is perfect for making beautiful and delicate sugar flowers. The gum agent makes the paste elastic and allows it to be rolled very thinly. There are a lot of wonderful pastes available from homemade recipes to ready-to-use commercial brands. As with other aspects of sugarcraft, gumpaste is sensitive to weather conditions and different environments, so I encourage you to try several varieties to find what will work best for you.

When working with gumpaste, use a small amount of cornstarch (cornflour) on your fingertips or your work surface if the paste feels sticky. Use a bit of vegetable shortening if the paste feels dry. When using cornstarch and shortening, use very small amounts to prevent the paste from drying out or becoming greasy and separating. Always keep your paste tightly sealed in a bag or container to prevent drying out. Homemade paste is best kept in the refrigerator when not in use for more than several days. Bring it to room temperature before using. Homemade paste can dry very quickly. If I need more working time for a specific flower, I will mix homemade paste 50/50 with commercial paste to slow down the drying time.

TYLOSE GUMPASTE

Adapted from a recipe created by Chef Nicholas Lodge, I've adjusted a few measurements to create paste that works well with my techniques. Makes about 2lb (900g) of gumpaste.

- 4½oz (125g) fresh or pasteurized egg whites
- 1lb 9½oz (725g) confectioner's (icing) sugar (+ extra for kneading)
- 1oz (25g) tylose powder
- ⅝oz (17g) vegetable shortening (white vegetable fat) (Crisco or alternative)

1. Place the egg whites and confectioner's sugar in a stand mixer fitted with the paddle attachment. Mix on low speed until blended.

2. Turn the mixer to medium-high for two full minutes. The mixture should be glossy and smooth like soft-peak meringue. If coloring the entire batch, add the gel color at this stage.

3. Scrape down the bowl and turn the mixer to low. Add the tylose powder until fully incorporated. Turn the mixer up to medium-high for about 30 seconds until the paste looks smooth.

4. Scrape the mixture out of the bowl onto a smooth surface sprinkled with some of the extra confectioner's sugar. Knead in all the vegetable shortening, adding more sugar if the paste feels sticky. The paste is ready when it feels smooth, and you can pinch it cleanly with your fingers.

5. Wrap the paste tightly in cling-wrap and then in a zip-top bag. Place in the refrigerator to mature for 24 hours if possible. When ready to use, allow the paste to come to room temperature. Cut off small pieces and knead until smooth, adding a bit of cornstarch (cornflour) or shortening if needed. Store the paste in the refrigerator for up to two months or in the freezer for up to six months.

COLORING GUMPASTE

Add gel color with a toothpick (cocktail stick) and knead the paste until the color is blended completely. The color will deepen a bit while it is resting but will get lighter as the paste dries. If desired, use disposable gloves to avoid staining your hands. To create pastel colors, make a small amount of the chosen color but in a darker shade than desired. Then keep adding white paste until you achieve the shade you want **(1)**. To make Petalsweet greens, start with moss green (Wilton Moss Green) or avocado (Americolor Gel Avocado). These colors are great on their own for some leaves, or add a bit of yellow (Americolor Gel Lemon Yellow) for a soft green. Add a bit of dark green (Americolor Gel Forest Green) to the base colors for a deep green that mixes well with rich colored flowers. For brown leaves, use ivory (Americolor Gel Ivory) so the leaves look light and delicate when dusted with oranges and browns **(2)**.

WIRING FLOWER CENTERS

Create a small hook to secure paste to a wire. For an open hook, grab the top of the wire with pliers and bend it over without closing the loop. For a closed hook as shown, squeeze the open hook closed with the pliers **(3)**. To attach paste to a wire, dab a little sugar glue on the hook, wiping off the excess so it is just damp. Insert the hook into the center of the ball of paste. Pinch a small amount of paste out of the bottom of the ball, turning the wire and pinching until the extra paste below the ball is quite thin. Hold on to the paste with your fingers and twist the wire quickly to break off the extra paste **(4)**. For a longer bud shape, insert the hook into the widest part of the bud. Gently roll the paste between your fingers to taper the paste down the wire until the desired length is reached. Twist the wire to break off any extra paste and gently roll the end between your fingers to smooth **(5)**.

WIRING PETALS & LEAVES

Once you have rolled your paste and cut your petal or leaf shape, dip the wire end into sugar glue and wipe off the excess. Hold the base of the petal or leaf between your thumb and finger with the groove facing up towards you. Gently insert the wire into the groove to get it started, and then continue a bit at a time, using your thumb over the top to feel the wire **(6)**. Once the wire is in the groove, gently press where the paste and wire come together to secure **(7)**. Alternatively, lay the petal or leaf on a foam pad with the groove side up and the base at the edge of the pad. Place your finger gently on the groove, and insert the wire a bit at a time. Secure the wire as described above.

FLORAL TAPE & FLOSS

Moss green and yellow-green floral tape are ideal for greenery or visible flower stems. For an all-white or pale arrangement, or to hide the stems, try white floral tape. You can always dust floral tape to enhance flowers or greenery. Use a tape cutter or craft knife to cut the tape to half width or narrower. Cut it to the desired length and stretch gently to release the gums in the tape. Pull it tightly to secure petals or leaves as you attach them to a stem. Use as little floral tape as possible to avoid bulkiness **(8)**. I use waxed dental floss to attach bunches of stamens, or to minimize bulk when adding a lot of petals. It can be pulled tightly without breaking, but hold it taut or it will unravel a bit. Always cover the floss with floral tape once the petals or stamens are secured.

BRUSHES & DUSTING

I recommend a mix of brushes for dusting. Flat, firm ones in sizes ⅛in (3mm) up to ¾in (2cm) are perfect for edging petals and leaves, and applying color in specific areas **(9)**. Use round, soft brushes ½in (1cm) up to 1in (2.5cm) to apply a soft blush and to blend shades, or add color across large petals quickly **(10)**. Lighten dust colors with cornstarch (cornflour) or white petal dust, and use a light touch. You can always add more color, but you can't take it away! Edge pastel colored petals with a slightly darker shade to make them look airy and delicate without saturating them. Practice any new colors on spare dried paste.

POLLEN

"Pollen" can add a realistic touch to flower centers and stamen tips **(11 and 12)**. Mix unflavored gelatin with petal dust until the desired color is achieved. Store in an airtight container. The most used colors are yellow, green, brown and black.

STEAMING & GLAZING

Gently steam your flowers and leaves to set the dust colors. The "dustiness" will disappear, and colors will blend like watercolors. Note that dust colors will deepen a bit when steamed. Hold flowers at least 6in (15cm) away from the steam and move them around constantly so no part absorbs too much moisture **(13)**. Steam for a few seconds at a time, until the flower no longer looks dry, but not shiny. Too long can cause flowers to become soft or fall apart. Dry completely before using. For shine, apply liquid leaf/confectioner's glaze sparingly with a small brush **(14)** or use spray glaze carefully (outdoors to prevent a sticky mess). Apply a very thin layer on paste that is dusted, steamed and completely dry. For less shine, mix the liquid glaze 50/50 with alcohol or glaze thinner before application. Drying time will vary depending on the environment so test a practice piece before glazing all your work. Severe humidity or wet weather may prevent the glaze from drying completely.

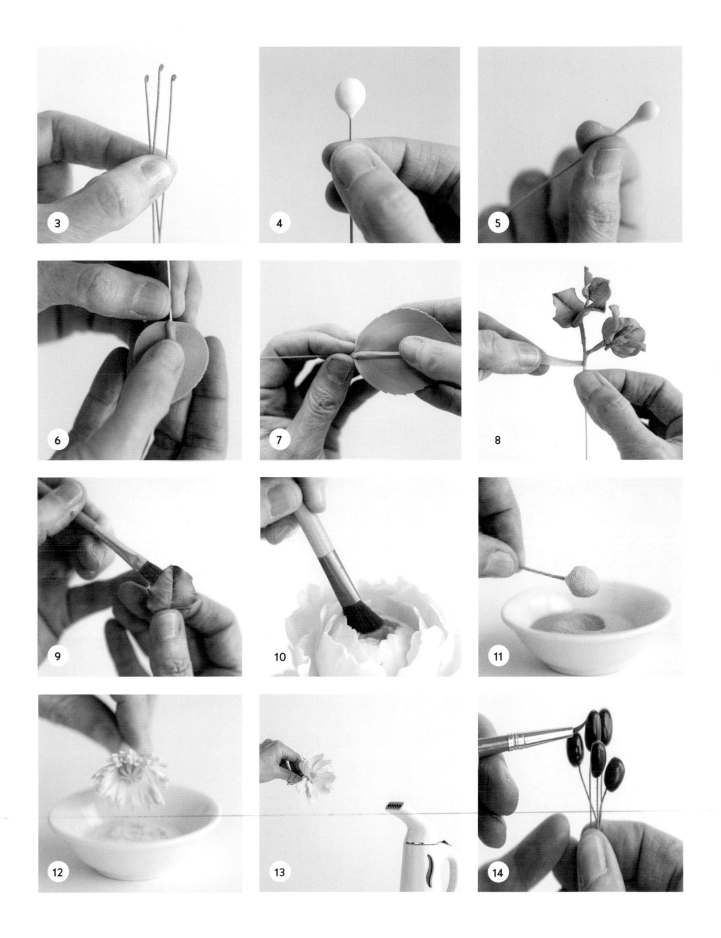

Staples & Fillers

This chapter features our favorite staples and fillers, including hydrangea, filler flowers, berries and greenery. We use them all to create our signature Petalsweet look, but we love them for their amazing functionality. Leaves and greenery provide a beautiful backdrop for focal flowers, and the fillers help to create lush, full arrangements by filling gaps between flowers and adding texture and visual interest.

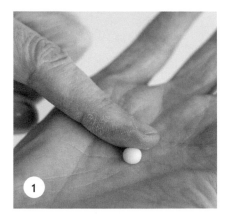

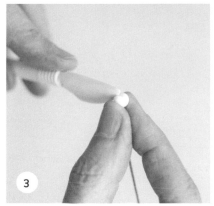

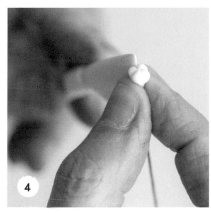

HYDRANGEA

SPECIFICS YOU WILL NEED

- Hydrangea flower cutter, 1½ x 1½in (4 x 4cm) (World of Sugar Art)
- Hydrangea flower single-sided veiner (World of Sugar Art)
- Hydrangea leaf cutter (World of Sugar Art)
- Hydrangea leaf single-sided veiner (World of Sugar Art)
- 26g green wire
- Knife tool
- Shallow cupped formers for flowers
- Hanging rack

- Acoustic "bumpy" foam
- Kiwi petal dust
- Moss Green petal dust
- Daffodil petal dust
- Magenta petal dust
- Confectioner's glaze (or leaf glaze)
- White paste
- Hydrangea green paste (Americolor Gel Avocado and Lemon Yellow)
- Leaf paste (Wilton Moss Green and Americolor Gel Avocado)

MAKE THE CENTERS

1. Roll a tiny ³⁄₁₆in (4mm) ball of white paste until it is smooth.

2. Attach neatly to 26g green hooked wire (see Getting Started).

3. Use a knife tool to make an indentation across the middle of the paste to create two halves.

4. Use the knife tool to make two more indentations dividing the halves into half again.

5. Make a center for each hydrangea flower you will be creating. Let them dry completely before adding petals.

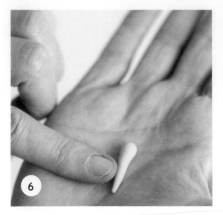

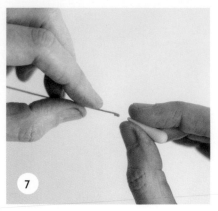

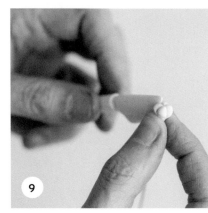

MAKE THE BUDS

6. Roll a small ball of pale green paste, ¼in (5mm) in diameter. Roll the bottom half of the ball into a tapered cone, leaving a bulbous tip.

7. Insert a hooked 26g green wire until the hook is in the middle of the widest part of the bud.

8. Thin and taper the base of the bud by rolling it between your fingers until the bud is ¾–1in (2–2.5cm) in length.

9. Use the knife tool to mark the top of the bud into quarters in the same way as the hydrangea centers.

10. For visual interest, make buds in a variety of sizes but keep them all small. Allow them to dry completely.

MAKE THE FLOWERS

11. Roll soft green paste thinly to ⅟₁₆in (2mm), keeping it covered if necessary to prevent it drying out. Press in spots all over the paste evenly with the hydrangea flower veiner.

12. Cut hydrangea flower shapes, centering the cutter over the veining. Keep the flowers covered to prevent drying.

13. Work with three to four flowers at a time and place on a foam pad. Thin the outer edges with a ball tool and go back with firmer pressure if a more ruffled flower is desired.

14. Apply a small amount of sugar glue on the underside of a hydrangea center.

15. Slide one of the hydrangea flowers up the wire.

16. Gently attach the center to the flower.

17. Turn the flower upside down and secure it to the center by pressing the base with your fingertips.

18. Hang most of the flowers upside down to dry (this will allow them to nestle more tightly together in an arrangement).

19. Dry some of the hydrangea flowers right-side up in a shallow cupped former to create some visual interest and use in layering the flowers over each other.

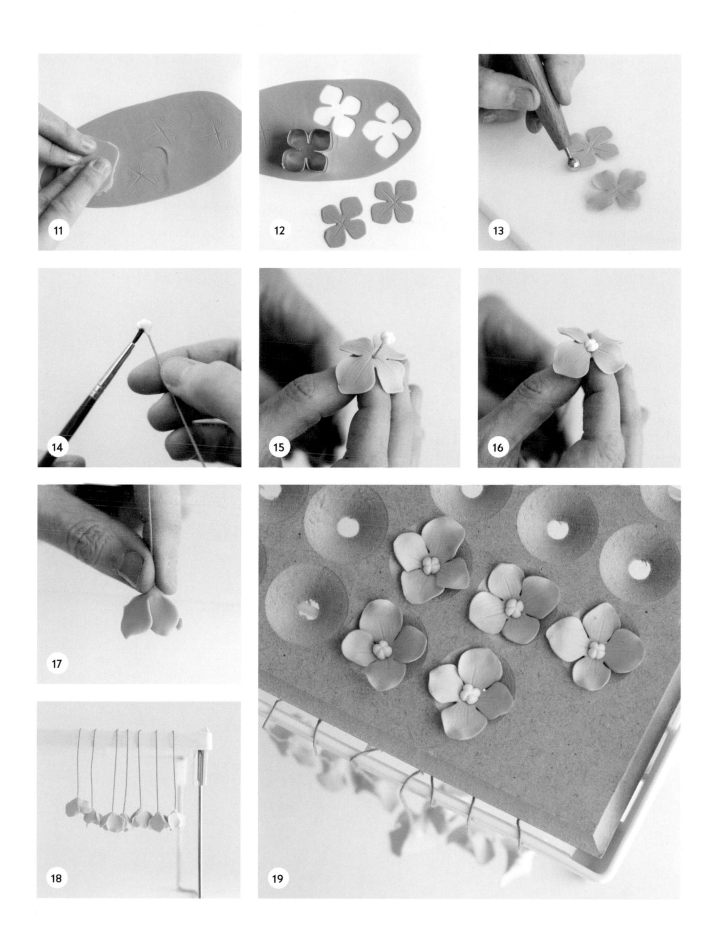

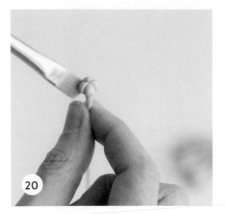
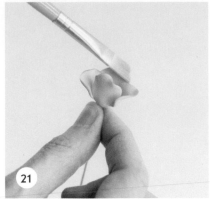
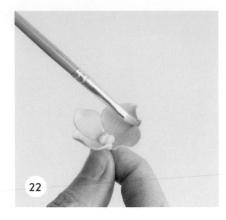

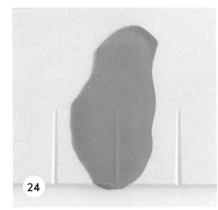
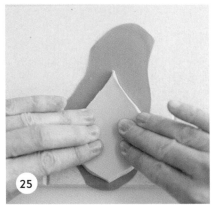

DUST THE BUDS AND FLOWERS

20. Dust Kiwi petal dust over the entire bud.

21. Dust Kiwi on the hydrangea flowers, working from the outer edges in towards the center, avoiding getting color on the white centers.

22. Add a bit of Magenta dust on random edges of the flowers if desired.

23. The closed hydrangea flowers fit together more tightly, but the open petals add some charm and dimension.

MAKE THE LEAVES

24. Roll the green leaf paste until moderately thin, to about ⅟₁₆in (2mm), on a groove board.

25. Press the paste evenly with the hydrangea leaf veiner, centering it over the groove.

26. Move the paste to a cutting surface and cut a hydrangea leaf.

27. Dip the end of a 26g green wire into sugar glue. Insert it about 1in (2.5cm) into the groove on the back of the leaf (see Getting Started).

28. Pinch the paste where the wire enters the leaf to secure it to the wire.

29. On a foam pad, thin the edges of the reverse side of the leaf with a ball tool. Repeat with heavier pressure on the edges to add movement.

30. Lay the leaf right-side up on a piece of foam to dry completely.

31. Dust the topside of the leaf with Moss Green dust, leaving the underside untouched.

32. Add a bit of Daffodil dust and Kiwi dust in small random splotches on the leaf.

33. Dust a tiny bit of Magenta on random parts of the edge of the leaf.

34. Steam the leaf for a few seconds to set the colors and let it dry (see Getting Started).

35. If desired, dab the topside of the leaf with a thin coat of confectioner's glaze or leaf glaze to create a nice shine. Let the leaves dry completely before using.

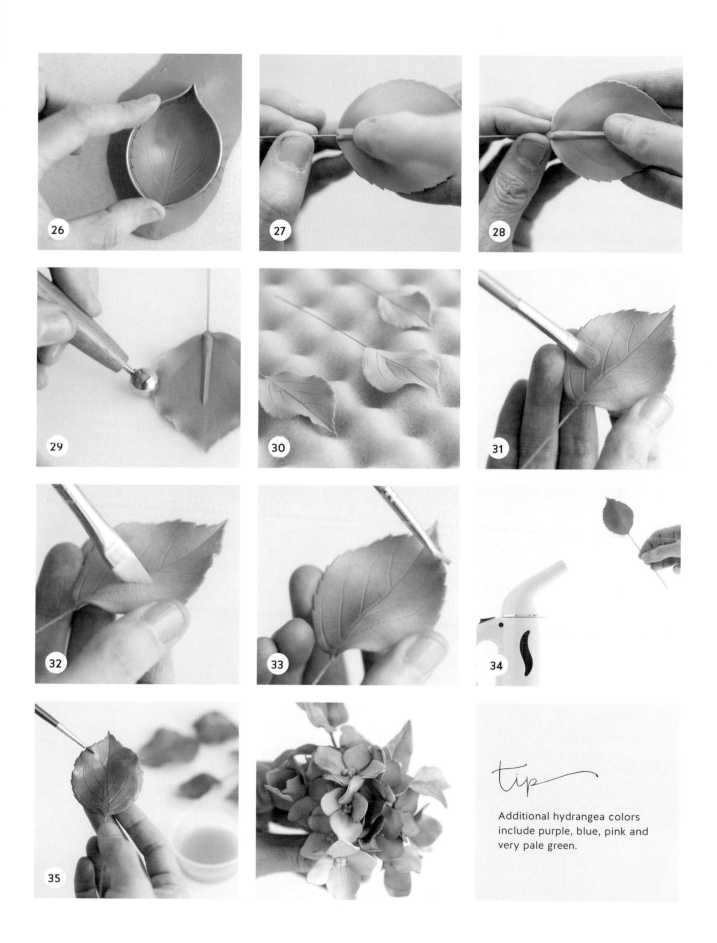

tip

Additional hydrangea colors include purple, blue, pink and very pale green.

FILLER FLOWERS

SPECIFICS YOU WILL NEED

· ·

- Cone tool
- Knife tool
- Small scissors
- 26g green wire
- 28g green wire
- 30g green wire
- 22g green wire
- Kiwi petal dust
- Moss Green petal dust
- Small amount of pale yellow soft royal icing (Americolor Gel Lemon Yellow)
- Small piping cone (bag)
- White paste
- Green paste (Wilton Moss Green)

MAKE THE FILLER FLOWERS

1. Roll a small ¼in (5mm) narrow cone of white paste, 1in (2.5cm) long.

2. Open the top with the cone tool, creating a ¼in (5mm) deep hole.

3. Using scissors, cut into the rim of the opening five times to create the petals.

4. Using your fingers, gently press the square corners of the petals to round them.

5. Flatten the petals firmly between your thumb and finger.

6. Turn the flower upside down on a foam pad and cup the underside of each petal by gently pressing with a small ball tool.

7. Slide a hooked 26g wire down through the center of the flower, just until the hook disappears out of sight.

8. Gently roll the base of the flower between your fingers to attach it neatly to the wire. Set in styrofoam to let it dry completely.

9. Color a small amount of soft royal icing pale yellow and spoon into a piping cone. Snip a tiny tip off the point with scissors. Pipe the centers of the flowers, filling the tiny center hole with icing and hiding the tops of the wires. Allow to dry completely before using.

MAKE THE FILLER FLOWER BUDS

10. Roll a tiny ³⁄₁₆in (4mm) ball of white paste until smooth, and attach neatly to a hooked 28g wire (see Getting Started).

11. Use a knife tool to make three indentations evenly around the top of the bud. Let it dry. Dust a tiny amount of Kiwi petal dust on the base of the bud to finish, and steam to set the color (see Getting Started).

MAKE THE LEAVES

12. Roll a tiny ³⁄₁₆in (4mm) ball of green paste into a cone and attach it to a hooked 30g wire, with the pointed end at the top. Flatten firmly between your thumb and finger.

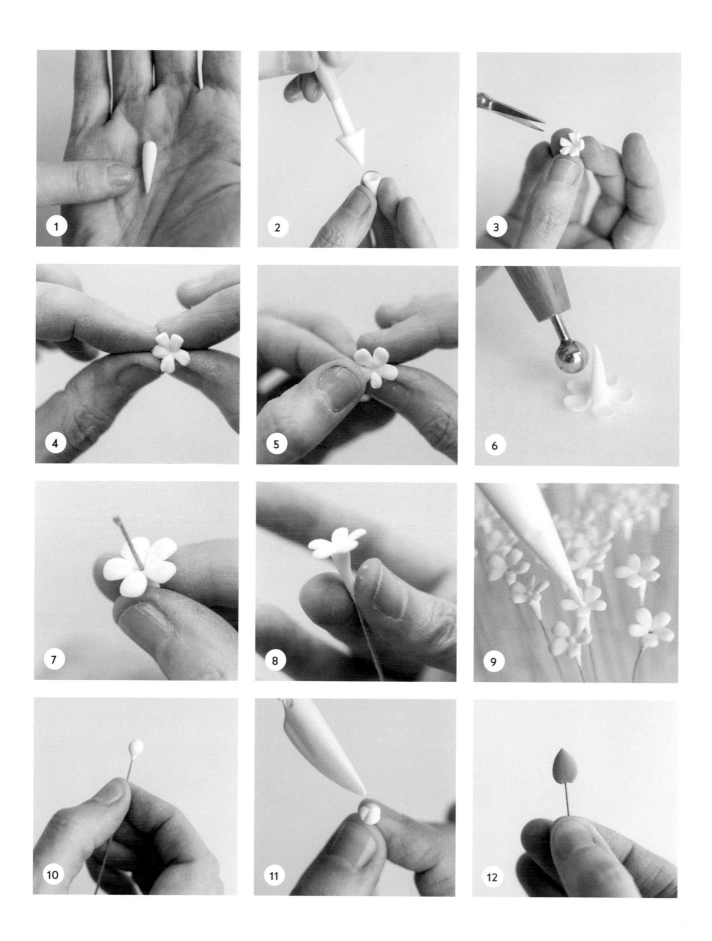

13. Lay the leaf on a foam pad and press on both sides of the wire with your fingertips, creating a center vein and the sides of the leaf.

14. Smooth and stretch the two sides with a ball tool to create the leaf shape. Pinch the leaf tip to finish. Let it dry completely.

15. Dust with Moss Green petal dust and finish with a tiny dab of confectioner's or leaf glaze (see Getting Started) for a bit of shine. Let the leaf dry before using.

MAKE THE ALL-PURPOSE BUDS

16. Roll a ½in (1cm) ball of white paste into a chunky cone shape, and attach to a 22g hooked wire.

17. Use a knife tool to create three indentations from the base of the bud to the tip, evenly spaced around the bud. Let it dry completely.

18. Dust the base of the bud and up through the indentations with Kiwi dust. Steam for a few seconds to set color and let dry before using. Make the buds in both green and white, and in a variety of small sizes.

FILLER FLOWER VARIATIONS

19. Make the filler flower the same way, up to using the ball tool. This time run the ball tool on the top side of the petals, gently stretching them.

20. Leave to dry and finish with a small drop of royal icing in the center.

21. Begin the filler flower the same way but cut only four petals. Flatten the petals between your thumb and finger and gently smooth and stretch with a ball tool.

22. If desired, gently pinch the outer tip of the petals.

23. Finish the flowers with a drop of royal icing in the center or brush the centers with petal dust.

tip

When gathering together the flowers into a bouquet, allow the pieces to all be at slightly different heights. This will make them look more natural.

GREENERY & BERRIES

SPECIFICS YOU WILL NEED

SIMPLE BERRIES

- Paste in berry colors
- 30g green and white wire
- Floral tape, green and white
- Star tool
- Petal dust in stem colors
- Alcohol
- Confectioner's glaze

BLUEBERRIES

- Blue paste (Americolor Gel Royal Blue + Black + a bit of Violet)
- Small scissors
- Dresden tool
- Wooden skewer, with flat and pointed ends
- 30g green wire
- White petal dust
- Cornstarch (cornflour)

GREENERY

- Leaves, see Additional Leaves
- 24g green or white wire (branches)
- 28g green wire (vines and tendrils)
- Floral tape, green, white and brown
- Petal dusts in greens, soft brown, grey and aubergine
- Wire cutters

MAKE SIMPLE BERRIES

1. Using your desired paste color, roll small balls or ovals of paste until smooth. Use photos of real berries for inspiration.

2. Dip the end of a 30g wire in sugar glue. Insert the wire through the paste until you feel the end poking out on the other side of the berry.

3. In another variation, insert the wire halfway into the berry and then press into the top of the paste with the star tool to create an indentation.

4. Dry in styrofoam by sticking the wires into the side of a dummy. Repeat until you have all your berries made. Leave to dry.

5. Dust the berries as desired, covering some completely with color. On others, create a blush of color on the sides using a flat brush. Steam to set the dust color and leave to dry (see Getting Started).

6. To create colored stems, use 30g white wire. Apply petal dust firmly with a flat brush and steam to set the color.

7. Using half-width floral tape, group berries in small bunches (odd numbers are best).

8. To create a branch, tape several bunches together and add small leaves if desired.

9. Brush on confectioner's glaze if your berries need a shiny finish. Leave to dry before using.

10. Add speckles to berries by loading a small paintbrush with a bit of gel color or petal dust mixed with alcohol. Tap the brush firmly over the berries to create the speckled effect.

11. Add speckles to leaves in the same way.

12. Create berries in any color and size to complement or add a pop of color to your arrangement.

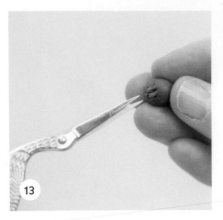

MAKE BLUEBERRIES

13. Roll a small ball of blue paste and snip three or four times into the top with small scissors, making shallow cuts.

14. Using the back of a Dresden tool, push the flaps of paste open to flatten against your finger, creating a ridge around the top of the berry. Try to make the ridge uneven and a bit messy looking.

15. Using the flat end of a wooden skewer, gently press it into the center of the berry. Dip a 30g green wire into sugar glue and insert the end into the base of the berry, being careful not to push it out through the top.

16. To make berries that have not split open on the top, roll smooth balls of paste and press into the top with the flat end of a wooden skewer and then the pointed tip of the skewer or a mini Celpin. Insert a wire as in step 15.

17. Let the berries dry and then steam to deepen the color. Let them dry again. Using white petal dust mixed with cornstarch (cornflour) on your fingers, roll and rub the berries to partially cover them. Use more on some and less on others for a natural look. Do not steam!

MAKE A BRANCH

18. Tape several leaves to a 24g wire to create a small branch. Repeat to create at least two more small branches. With small leaves, you can use a finer wire for the branches. Larger, heavier leaves can make the branch bend too easily, so plan ahead for how you will use the branches in your design.

19. Use one of the small branches as the main branch and tape the other two branches to it, spacing them unevenly down the wire. Tape down the wire to cover completely.

20. You can use petal dusts to add color and depth to the floral tape on the branches, especially if you are using white floral tape. I use greens, soft browns, grey and aubergine petal dust on my branches, depending on the leaves. Steam the branch after dusting to help set the colors and leave to dry before using.

21. For another variation, tape small single buds or groups of berries on a branch between leaves.

TAPING GREENERY

22. Gather your individual leaves. Using half-width or quarter-width floral tape, wrap down the wire of one leaf up to 1in (2.5cm). Attach a second leaf at its base wrapping over the join with tape.

23. Continue adding leaves opposite each other spaced down the stem.

24. Make the greenery stem any length desired. Use wire cutters as you go to clip excess wires of attached leaves to keep the center stem from getting too bulky.

25. For another variation, attach leaves spaced unevenly down the center stem.

26. For a delicate branch and tendril, twist half-width floral tape between your fingers to create a tendril. Tape the tendril to a 28g wire and add a few very small leaves spaced unevenly down the center stem.

27. For another variation, tape leaves together in small groups and use as fillers in between and around flowers.

ADDITIONAL LEAVES

Beautiful leaves are great for framing and bringing life to flowers and arrangements. Don't worry about having the exact leaves to match all your flowers, Keep your favorites on hand, and make a specific leaf when you need it. Follow the wiring instructions for the hydrangea leaves, but press the wired paste between the silicone veiners listed here before drying and finishing.

MAGNOLIA LEAVES (1)

- Moss green paste/26g wire
- Leaf cutters large (Gardenia leaf cutters by Sugar Art Studio)
- Leaf cutter small (Dahlia petal cutter by World of Sugar Art)
- Leaf veiner (Large rose leaf veiner by SK Great Impressions)
- Moss Green + Kiwi petal dusts
- Steam to finish

ROSE LEAVES (2)

- Moss green paste/26g wire
- Leaf cutters (Rose leaf cutters by World of Sugar Art)
- Multi-purpose leaf veiner (Sunflower Sugar Art)
- Moss Green petal dust on leaf
- Moss Green + Holly petal dusts in center vein
- Magenta petal dust on a few spots on edges
- Steam to finish

BOUGAINVILLEA LEAVES (3)

- Yellow-green paste/30g wire
- Leaf cutters: ½ x ⅝in (1 x 1.5cm), ¾ x ⅞in (2 x 2.3cm), ⅞ x 1in (2.3 x 2.5cm) rose petal cutters
- Leaf veiner (Large rose leaf veiner by SK Great Impressions)
- Kiwi petal dust
- Steam to finish

DOGWOOD LEAVES (4)

- Yellow-green paste/26g wire
- Teardrop shape, 1¼ x ⅝in (3 x 1.5cm) cut with cutting wheel
- Dogwood leaf veiner (First Impressions Molds)
- Moss Green + Kiwi petal dusts
- Steam to finish

EUCALYPTUS (5)

- Grey-green paste/30g white wire
- Circle cutters, 1in (2.5cm), 1¼in (3cm) and 1½in (4cm)
- Use ball tool to stretch paste a bit up through the center
- Veiner (Large rose leaf veiner by SK Great Impressions)
- Eucalyptus, Moss Green and a touch of Chocolate Brown petal dusts
- Tape leaves in opposite pairs
- Steam to finish

OLIVE LEAVES (6)

- Moss green paste + ivory with a touch of green paste/30g white wire
- Leaf cutter: 2¼in (5.5cm) long dahlia petal cutter narrowed to ½in (1cm) width
- Leaf veiner (Multi-purpose leaf veiner by First Impressions Molds)
- Use Moss Green petal dust on top of leaf only
- Steam to finish

MULTI-PURPOSE GREENERY LEAVES (7)

- Moss green or moss/forest green paste/28g or 30g wire
- Leaf cutters (Dahlia petal cutters by World of Sugar Art, using pointed end at the top)
- Leaf veiner (Multi-purpose leaf veiner by First Impressions Molds)
- Trace mold with cutting wheel for additional leaf shapes
- Kiwi + Moss Green petal dusts (lighter leaves) or Moss Green + Foliage petal dusts (darker leaves)
- Steam to finish

SPRING LEAVES (8)

- Yellow-green paste/30g white wire
- Leaf cutter, ⅞ x 1in (2.3 x 2.5cm), 1⅛ x 1⅜in (3 x 3.5cm), rose petal cutter using point at the top
- Briar Rose leaf veiner (SK Great Impressions)
- Kiwi dust, for leaf
- Moss Green and Donut petal dusts, for some edges and base of leaf
- Tape together with white floral tape to form small branches
- Use the same dust colors on the floral tape
- Steam to finish

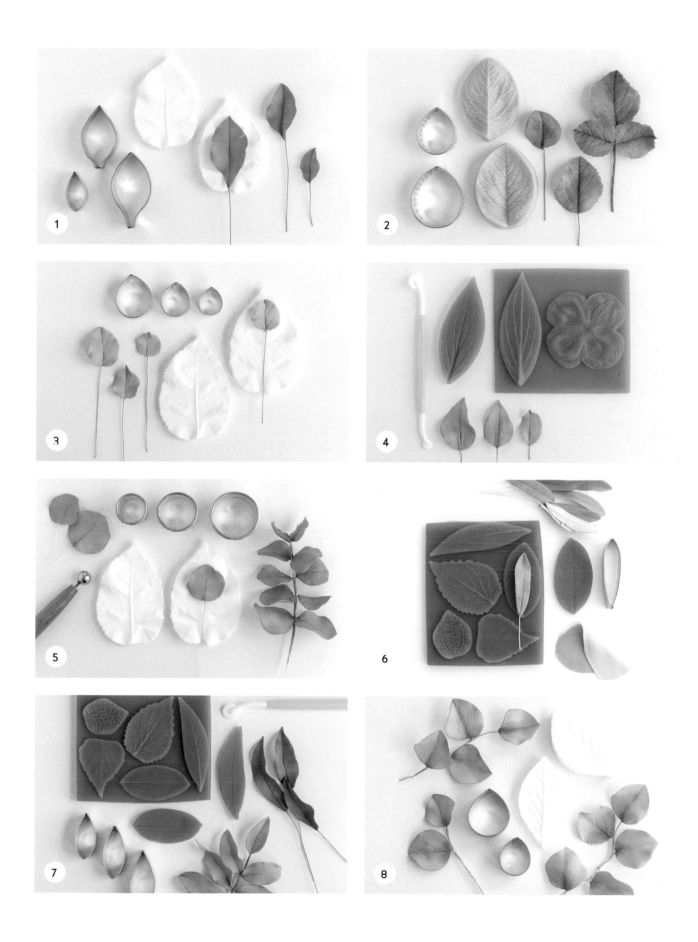

THE Flowers

Bougainvillea

Sometimes referred to as the "paper flower", it's not the tiny buds and flowers that make bougainvillea so recognizable, but the colorful papery bracts. With varieties that range from white to deep magenta, this flower is a great way to add vibrant hues to your arrangements. Use small clusters of the bracts and buds as fillers to add a little pop of color, or tape together a few long stems to add dimension and movement to highlight your focal flowers.

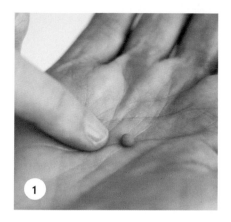

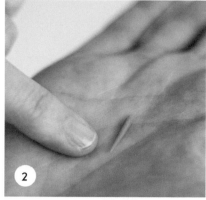

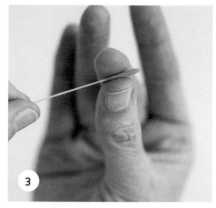

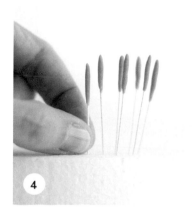

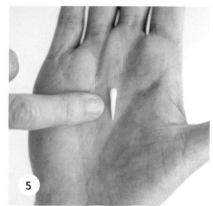

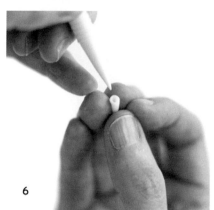

SPECIFICS YOU WILL NEED

· Purple paste (Wilton Violet + Pink)
· White paste
· Rose petal cutters in four sizes: ½ x ⅝in (1 x 1.5cm), ¾ x ⅞in (2 x 2.3cm), ⅞ x 1in (2.3 x 2.5cm), 1⅛ x 1⅜in (3 x 3.5cm) (World of Sugar Art)
· Bougainvillea bract veiners (Squires Kitchen Shop or Marcel Veldbloem Flower Veiners)
· 30g and 24g white wire
· Scribing tool
· Acoustic "bumpy" foam
· Floral tape, white and tan/beige
· Lilac, Cosmos, Chocolate Brown and Moss Green petal dusts
· Bougainvillea leaves (see Additional Leaves)

MAKE THE CENTERS

1. To make the simple bud centers, cut 30g wire into 2in (5cm) lengths. Roll a tiny ball of purple paste, ⅛in (3mm) in diameter.

2. Roll the ball into a thin rope about ¾in (2cm) long.

3. Insert a wire and roll gently between fingers to attach paste smoothly to it.

4. Set the center in styrofoam to dry completely. You will need two or three buds per cluster of bracts.

5. To make the bloomed bud centers, roll a ¼in (5mm) ball of white paste into a narrow cone.

6. Press ⅛in (3mm) into the top of the cone with the pointed end of a scribing tool.

7. Using small scissors, snip to create seven or eight petals.

8. Gently flatten the petals between your thumb and finger.

9. Slide a 30g wire halfway up into the base of the cone. Secure to the wire by gently rolling the cone between your fingers.

10. Set in styrofoam and very gently squeeze the neck of the flower to open the petals.

11. Create a tiny opening in the center of the flower with the scribing tool, then allow it to dry completely.

MAKE THE BRACTS

12. Roll purple paste thinly, to about ⅛in (2mm) on a groove board.

13. Using the four sizes of rose petal cutters, cut the bract shapes with the point of the cutter at the top.

14. Dip a 30g wire in sugar glue and insert it ⅜in (1cm) into the groove. Secure at the base with your fingers.

15. Thin the edges of the bracts with a ball tool on a foam pad and press in a veiner.

16. On the reverse side of the bracts, use a ball tool on a foam pad to add movement to the outer edges.

17. Dry the bracts in the acoustic "bumpy" foam with most of them face down and slightly curling backwards.

18. Lay some bracts on top of the foam bumps to dry flatter and some in the dips to make them more cupped, for a good mixture of shapes to tape together in clusters.

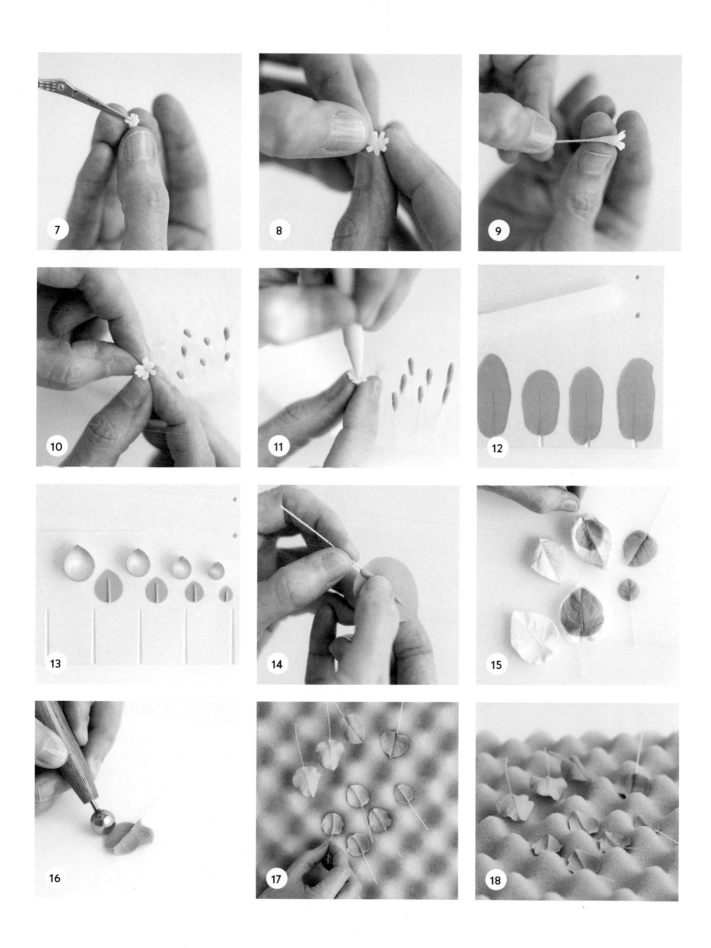

DUST THE BOUGAINVILLEA

19. Dust the simple bud centers with a mixture of Lilac and Cosmos dust, making them a bit darker at the base.

20. Dust the base and neck of the bloomed bud centers, leaving the tops white.

21. Dust around the edges of the bracts, drawing the color a little towards the center. Add a bit more color at the base of the bracts near the wires.

ASSEMBLE THE BOUGAINVILLEA

22. Using white floral tape, attach three simple buds together at their bases, varying their heights slightly.

23. Using tan/beige floral tape, attach two or three same-size bracts so they are curling away from the buds. Then tape about 1in (2.5cm) down the length of the wires. This is a cluster.

24. Use a mixture of two simple buds and one bloomed bud to make another cluster with two or three same-size bracts.

25. Continue taping together clusters using a mix of both types of buds with the bracts. Set aside a few of the smallest bracts to use as the start of a stem. Steam all the clusters and bracts and allow them to dry before taping them into a stem. Clusters can also be used on their own as fillers between other flowers if you don't have space for a full stem.

26. Using a 24g white wire as a base, begin by taping two of the smallest bracts to the end of the wire. Tape about ¾in (2cm) down the length of the wire and add a small cluster. Tape down another 1in (2.5cm) and add a second cluster.

27. Add a couple of small single bougainvillea leaves.

28. Tape down the wire and add a few more clusters, gradually increasing the size of the bracts.

29. Continue adding clusters and leaves to create the stem length desired. Trim off a few wires as you go to prevent the main stem from getting too bulky.

30. Dust along the floral tape at the base of the clusters and leaves with a pale mixture of Moss Green and a tiny bit of Chocolate Brown petal dusts. Quickly steam to set the stem colors and allow them to dry before using.

33

Miniature Daisy

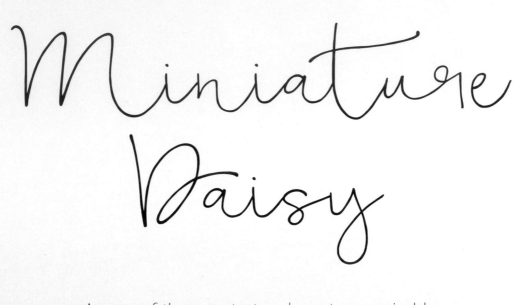

As one of the sweetest and most recognizable flowers that has ever bloomed, daisies are a happy favorite for many, with an enduring quality that evokes feelings of goodness and purity. And in an adorable miniature form, they are a perfect filler flower and little pop of color for summer arrangements. Make them in a variety of open and closed stages for a more organic feel, and don't forget to include a few of the sweet buds.

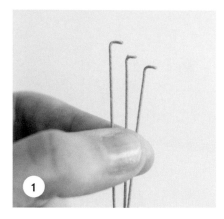

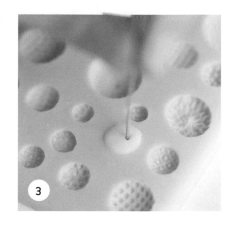

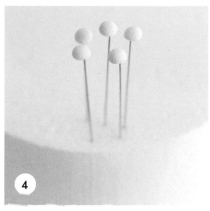

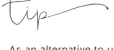

tip

As an alternative to using the center mold, roll ¼in (5mm) balls of yellow paste, attach to a hooked 26g wire and leave to dry. Continue making the daisies as described.

SPECIFICS YOU WILL NEED

- Yellow paste (Americolor Gel Lemon Yellow)
- Yellow-green paste (Wilton Moss Green + Americolor Gel Lemon Yellow)
- White paste
- Daisy cutter: 1¼in (3cm) 12-petal Gerbera Daisy cutters (World of Sugar Art)
- Daisy bud cutter: ¾in (2cm) 8-petal Daisy and Mum cutters (World of Sugar Art)
- Calyx cutter: ⅝in (1.5cm) 6-petal cutter N7 (Orchard Products)
- JEM veining tool
- Dresden tool
- 26g and 28g green wire
- Assorted flower center mold (First Impressions Molds)
- Yellow gelatin "pollen" mixture (see Getting Started)
- Moss Green and Kiwi petal dusts

MAKE THE CENTERS

1. Use pliers to create a tiny closed hook in a 26g wire. Bend the wire 90 degrees just below the hook to create an "L" shape at the end of the wire.

2. Roll a small ball of yellow paste and gently press into the flower center mold. I've used two sizes here: ¼in (5mm) and ⅜in (8mm).

3. Dip the hook in sugar glue and insert into the back of the paste in the mold. Pinch the paste around the wire to secure, and gently lift out the center from the mold.

4. Let the centers dry overnight.

5. Brush the tops of the centers with sugar glue and dip in yellow pollen mixture. Let them dry before using.

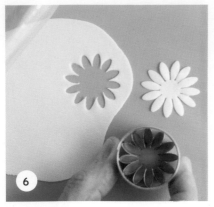

MAKE THE PETALS

6. Roll white paste thinly and keep it in a petal protector to prevent drying. Cut a 1¼in (3cm) 12-petal daisy shape.

7. On a foam pad with a ball tool, thin the outer tips and widen the petals a bit.

8. Using the JEM veining tool, vein the center of each petal.

9. Cup some of the petals by stroking firmly down the middle with the Dresden tool.

10. Brush glue in the center of the petal and slide it up from the bottom of the wire to attach it to the center.

11. Make and attach a second petal slightly offset from the first to create a fuller looking double daisy. Leave to dry in various formations (hanging versus upright) to create flowers at different stages of opening. Encourage some of the petals to close around the center or curl away from the center.

12. Using a small brush, dust Moss Green petal dust around the flower center at the base of the petals. Steam to set the dust color. Add a calyx to the base, if desired, by following the instructions in steps 16 and 17.

MAKE THE BUDS

13. Roll a ¼in (5mm) ball of white paste and attach it to a 28g hooked wire. Leave to dry.

14. Roll white paste thinly and cut a ¾in (2cm) 8-petal daisy shape. On a foam pad, thin the edges with a ball tool and cup the petals with the Dresden tool.

15. Brush glue on the petals and the bud center and wrap with the petals, covering the base. Wrap with a second daisy shape if desired, leaving the tips of the second petals open if you wish. Make a mixture of single and double buds.

16. Roll yellow-green paste thinly and cut a ⅝in (1.5cm) calyx shape. On a foam pad, widen the sections a bit with the ball tool and then pinch the tips. Attach to the base of the bud with a small amount of glue. Leave to dry.

17. Dust the calyx with Kiwi petal dust, extending the color on to the base of the bud. Steam to set the color and leave to dry before using.

Dogwood

A springtime favorite, dogwoods are among the first of the trees to bloom, attracting admiration with their magnificent display of flowers. The beautiful bracts are found in shades of white and pink, all the way to scarlet. Have fun with the distinct notches, curling some more than others, and try different petal dusts to color them, including green, champagne and burgundy. They are perfect as a secondary flower tucked into an arrangement, or tape a few together with some leaves to create a delicate branch, falling away from the edge of a cake.

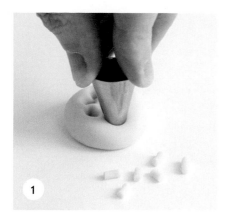

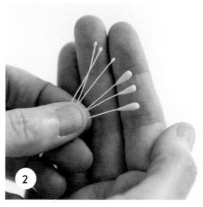

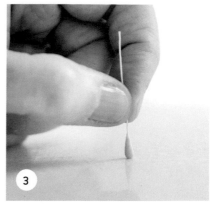

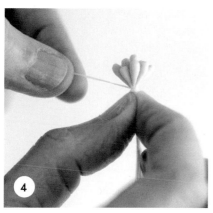

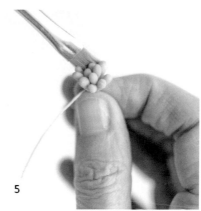

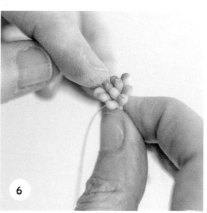

SPECIFICS YOU WILL NEED

···

- Pale green paste (Americolor Gel Avocado)
- White paste
- 30g white wire
- Dogwood bract cutters: 1⅜ x 1⅝in (3.5 x 4.3cm) rose petal cutter (World of Sugar Art)
- Dogwood bract veiner (First Impressions Molds)
- Dresden tool
- Round piping tip (nozzle), Wilton no.5
- Seed head stamens, small
- Waxed dental floss
- Floral tape, tan/beige
- Kiwi, Daffodil, Burgundy and Champagne petal dusts
- Magenta and Pink petal dusts, for a pink flower

MAKE THE FLOWER CLUSTER

1. Roll a 1in (2.5cm) ball of pale green paste into ⅕in (5mm) thickness. Using a no.5 piping tip, cut pieces of paste by twisting the tip down into and through the paste. Pop them out from the top of the piping tip with a toothpick (cocktail stick) or wire.

2. Roll the pieces to create narrow cone shapes. Dab seed head stamens in sugar glue and cover them with the pieces of paste, tapering the bases to the filaments.

3. Gently tap the tips on a firm surface to make them flat. Make 12–15 per flower cluster and leave to dry overnight.

4. Using waxed dental floss, wrap the pieces together at the base, forming the flower cluster. Leave the floss attached while dusting in the next step. You will use the floss to attach the bracts as well.

5. Dust the flower cluster with Kiwi petal dust.

6. With your fingertip, press Daffodil dust on the top of some of the pieces of the cluster. If desired, dab a bit of Burgundy on some of the tips as well. Steam to set the colors and leave to dry for a few minutes before adding the bracts.

MAKE THE BRACTS

7. I've used two bract shapes, one a bit narrower and one a bit wider. Both are made using a 1⅜ x 1⅝in (3.5 x 4.3cm) rose petal cutter. Press the cutter on the sides to make it narrower. Press down the top to make it wider. Use the same cutter for all of the bracts in a flower, or use two of each shape per flower.

8. Roll white paste thinly on a groove board and cut the bract shape.

9. Insert a 30g white wire ½in (1cm) into the bract and secure at the base.

10. Using a ball tool on a foam pad, thin the edges and then press in the veiner.

11. On a foam pad, work on the reverse of the petal. Use the Dresden tool along the outer edges to curl some of the edges back.

12. To make the dogwood's distinct notch, keep the petal face down. Push back a bit of the paste in the center of the top edge with the JEM tool or the tip of a small paintbrush. Make some notches larger than others for variety.

13. For a younger, just opening flower, dry two bracts over the end of a modeling tool, cupping the bases over the neck of the tool. Dry the remaining two bracts flat on foam.

14. For an open flower, dry all four bracts on the foam. To help ensure they fit together well, keep the bases of the bracts neat and smooth. If needed, you can loosely tape the bracts to the center once they are set but not dry. Let the bracts then dry completely before dismantling, dusting and re-assembling them.

FINISH THE FLOWER

15. Dust the notch with a bit of Kiwi petal dust. I also like to use a bit of Champagne and/or Burgundy dust on some of the notches for a flower that looks a bit more aged.

16. Using the waxed dental floss, attach the first two bracts just under the flower cluster, positioning them opposite each other.

17. Add the remaining two bracts underneath the first two, opposite each other. Tape over the floss and down over the filaments with tan/beige floral tape to create a single stem. If desired, dust a small amount of Kiwi at the base of the petals. Steam to set the dust colors and leave to dry before using.

18. For a pink version, dust over most of the petal surface with a mixture of Magenta and Pink dusts, leaving some paste white below the notches or at the base of the bracts. Add a deeper version of the same color around the outer edges. Steam the bracts and leave to dry before assembling the flower.

Tulips

Beautiful harbingers of springtime, cherished for their bright colors and cup-shaped flowers, I love tulips. The simple varieties have such clean lines, and the parrot tulips' wavy, twisted petals and bright striations are a stand out favorite. While simple tulips are easy to add to arrangements in a bunch or as a larger filler flower, the flamboyance of a parrot tulip can sometimes overwhelm a design. I simplified the dusting for them here so they can be mixed easily with other flowers. Once you are comfortable with the application of the petal dust, it's easy to use more to create a flashier variety.

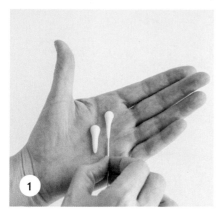

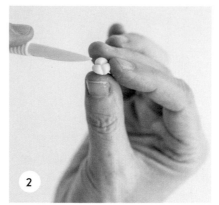

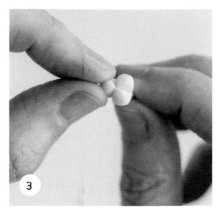

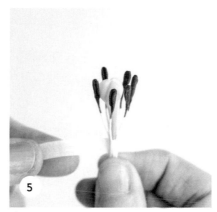

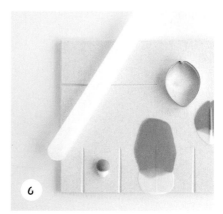

SIMPLE TULIP

SPECIFICS YOU WILL NEED

....

- Pale yellow paste (Americolor Gel Lemon Yellow)
- Purple paste (Wilton Violet + Pink)
- White paste
- Tulip petal cutter, 1¾ x 2¼in (4.5 x 5.5cm) (World of Sugar Art)
- Two tulip petal veiners (World of Sugar Art or Sunflower Sugar Art)
- 20g and 30g white wire
- JEM veining tool
- Dresden tool
- Floral tape, white and green
- Waxed dental floss
- Brown-tipped stamens (World of Sugar Art)
- Wooden skewer
- Half egg chocolate mold with six cavities, 1¾ x 2⅜in (4.5 x 6.7cm) (CK Products or Country Kitchen Sweet Art)
- Lilac, Daffodil and Kiwi petal dusts

MAKE THE CENTER

1. Roll a ⅜in (8mm) ball of pale-yellow paste into a 1in (2.5cm) long cone with a bulbous end and attach it to a hooked 20g wire, smoothing and tapering the end to secure it.

2. Using the knife tool, make three evenly spaced indentations around the top.

3. Gently pinch the three sections with your fingertips to narrow them a little. Set the center aside to dry completely.

4. Dust with pale Kiwi dust up from the base to the bulbous top. Add a bit of pale Daffodil all over the top. Steam to set the colors and allow to dry before using.

5. Using white floral tape, attach six brown-tipped stamens equally spaced around the base, so the tips of the stamens are about the same height as the center. In some tulip varieties, the stamens are shorter than the center, but I prefer them a bit longer for added elegance.

MAKE THE PETALS

6. To make the inner petals, press together a ½in (1cm) ball of white or cream-colored paste with a ⅜in (1.5cm) ball of your chosen tulip color (purple shown here). Roll the paste thinly on a groove board and cut the tulip petal with the cutter. Petals can also be made with a solid color of paste if you prefer.

7. Dip a 30g white wire in sugar glue and insert it ½in (1cm) into the groove, securing it at the base.

8. Thin the petal edges with a ball tool on a foam pad, and press the wired petal in between the two veiners. Be sure to line up the center of the petal along the center veining.

9. To accentuate the veining on the outer edges, gently roll sections of the petal with a JEM no.12 tool, following the direction of the veins while not disturbing the center vein. Use gentle pressure to avoid stretching the petal too much. This extra veining can be used on the inside or outside of the petal.

10. Lay the petal with the reverse side over a wooden skewer, lining the skewer underneath the center vein of the petal. Gently smooth over the top two thirds of the center of the petal with your fingers.

11. Use the wide end of a Dresden tool to curl in the left and right edges of the top half of the petal, and then use a small ball tool to cup the tips on both sides of the center vein.

12. Lay the petal in a 1¾ x 2⅝in (4.5 x 6.7cm) egg former, pressing the whole petal into the opening with the bottom edge of the petal into the *wide* end of the egg. The center vein will fold up on the inside in the top half of the petal. Gently press the wire to the shape of the former to give the petals a cupped shape base, and to help them all fit together nicely once dry. Make three inner petals per tulip. Allow them to dry completely.

13. Repeat the same process for the outer petals but stretch them in height and width by ¼in (5mm) before pressing them in the veiner, adding the center vein, and curling the edges with the Dresden tool.

14. Lay the petals in the egg former in the same way as the inner petals, with the base of the petals smoothed into the wide end of the egg former. If a more open petal is desired, press the petal into the side and base of the egg former, encouraging the petal edge over the edge of the egg shape (as shown). Make three outer petals per tulip. Allow them to dry completely.

DUST THE PETALS

15. Dust Lilac petal dust around the edges of the purple part of the petals to define them, leaving the white base undusted. Add a bit more down into the center vein from the top edge. For solid color tulips, a deeper color than the paste can also be brushed upwards from the base, to about ¼–½in (5–10mm) up the outside of the petal. For more realism, dust a small amount of Kiwi at the base of the petals and a few strokes coming up the center vein. The addition of the green is great for white or other pale colored tulips.

ASSEMBLE THE TULIP

16. Using waxed dental floss, attach the inner petals equally spaced around the center. Line up the base of the petal at the base of the tulip center.

17. Attach the three outer petals so they overlap the gaps between the first layer petals. Once all the petals are attached, cover the dental floss with white or green floral tape and tape all the way down the stem to cover the wires. Steam to set the petal dust and allow to dry before using.

18. If desired, add an additional layer or two of the larger, *outer* petals to make a Double Tulip as shown.

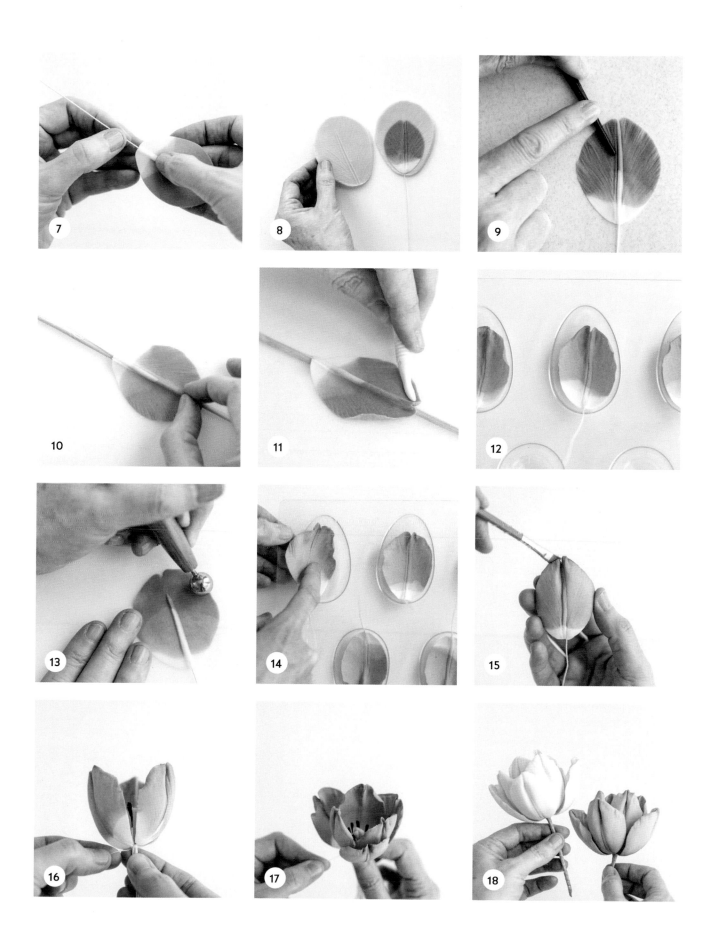

PARROT TULIP

SPECIFICS YOU WILL NEED

- Yellow paste (Americolor Gel Lemon Yellow)
- Yellow-green paste (Wilton Moss Green + Americolor Gel Lemon Yellow), for the leaves
- 20g and 26g white wire
- 26g green wire, for leaves
- Tulip petal cutter: 2⅛ x 2⅞in (5.4 x 7.5cm) rose petal cutter
- Calyx cutter, 1¾in (4.5cm)
- Two tulip petal veiners (Sunflower Sugar Art or World of Sugar Art)
- Corn husk veiner, for leaves (World of Sugar Art)
- Dresden tool
- Half egg chocolate mold, 1¾ x 2⅝in (4.5 x 6.7cm) (CK Products, Country Kitchen Sweet Art or Amazon)
- Cutting wheel
- Daffodil, Kiwi, Moss Green and Amethyst petal dusts
- Waxed dental floss
- Brown-tipped stamens (World of Sugar Art)
- Floral tape, green and white

MAKE THE CENTER AND PETALS

1. Refer to the instructions in steps 1–5 in Simple Tulip to make the tulip center in pale yellow or pale green. Then to make the petals, roll yellow paste thinly on a groove board and cut a 2⅛ x 2⅞in (5.4 x 7.5cm) petal. Insert a 26g white wire up to ½in (1cm) and secure at the base.

2. Working on firm surface, use the pointed tip of a 1¾in (4.5cm) calyx cutter to press into the outer edges and make cuts along the top and sides of the petal.

3. Press the petal between the veiners, especially along the outer edges of the petal to smooth any bumps.

4. Using small scissors, snip into the edges of a few sections of the petal.

5. On a foam pad with the Dresden tool, use moderate pressure to pull out sections of the petal edges.

6. Use the Dresden tool to curl and cup the outer edges with short strokes from the edge of the petal towards the middle. Make some strokes longer than others.

7. Center and lay the petal over a wooden skewer and gently press the paste to conform to the skewer. This will create a strong central vein on the reverse of the petal.

8. Lay the petal in a 1¾ x 2⅝in (4.5 x 6.7cm) egg former to dry. Press the base of the petal into the side of the former to keep it cupped, but encourage the outer right edge of the petal to lay over the edge of the former. The cupped base will help the two layers of petals fit together well. Gently press on the wire to conform it to the curved shape of the former as well.

9. To prevent a harsh crease on the petal, tuck a small piece of tissue underneath the petal to soften the bend. Use your fingers or a tool to curl some of the petal edges in towards the center and some of the bits out to make them more open.

10. Vary how the petals lay in the former, with left, right and top edges spilling out over the top of the former. This will give the illusion of more petal movement when the flower is taped together. Make six petals. Leave to dry completely.

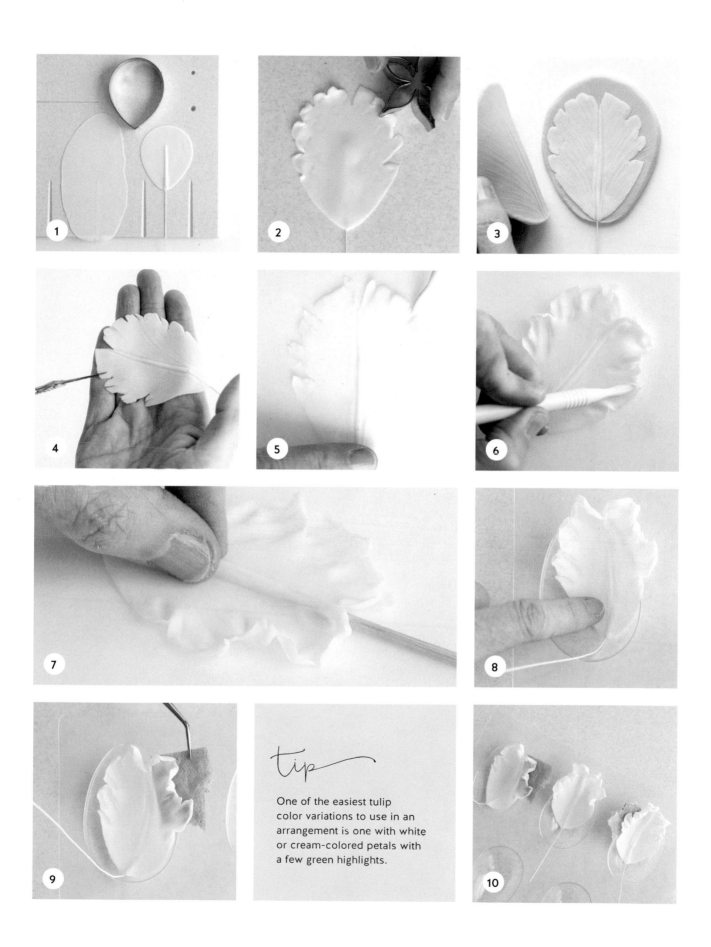

One of the easiest tulip color variations to use in an arrangement is one with white or cream-colored petals with a few green highlights.

DUST THE PETALS

11. Use Daffodil petal dust to create strokes of color from the base of the petals upwards alongside the center vein. Repeat on the outside of the petal.

12. Use strokes of Kiwi and Moss Green dust from the base going in and alongside the center vein. Again, repeat on the outside of the petal.

13. Use Amethyst dust in short strokes to define some of the outer edges. Add a few light strokes of the same color from the base of the petal up and alongside the green strokes from the previous step.

ASSEMBLE THE TULIP

14. Using waxed dental floss, attach three petals equally spaced around the center with the base of the petals aligned with the base of the stamens.

15. Attach the remaining three petals in a second layer, filling the gaps between the petals of the previous layer. Wrap over the floss and all the wires with floral tape to create a single stem. Steam to set the dust color and leave to dry before using.

16. Parrot tulips can be multi-colored or a solid color. Use photos for additional color inspiration.

MAKE THE LEAVES

17. Mix pale moss green paste with a bit of yellow paste. Roll paste thinly on a groove board. While it is on the board, gently stroke down the paste from top to bottom with a corn husk veiner. Keep your fingers and the veiner flat to avoid tearing the paste. The veining should be subtle. Cut a narrow leaf shape approximately 1½in wide by 5in tall (4 x 12.5cm) with a cutting wheel. Insert a 26g green wire up to 1in (2.5cm) into the leaf and secure at the base.

18. On a foam pad with a ball tool, work on the back of the leaf and thin the edges. Gently fold or twist the leaf to give it some shape and lay it on the foam to dry.

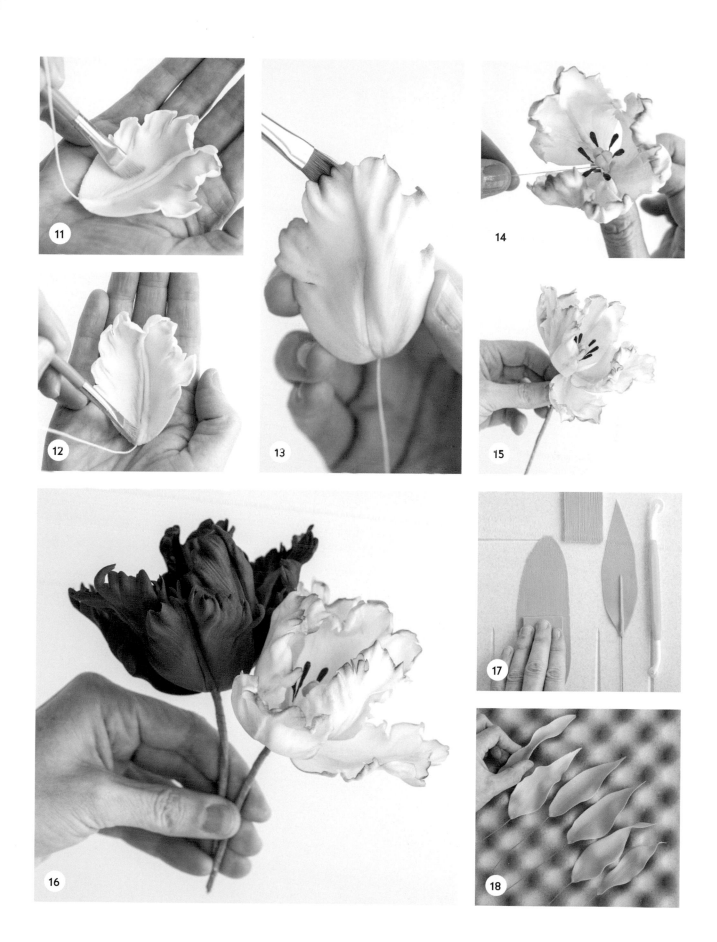

Gardenia

Originally found only in China and Japan, there are now over 200 different species of gardenia throughout the world. Fragile and elegant, the cut flowers don't last very long, so we are lucky to be able to make them in sugar! With their beautiful creamy petals, clean lines, and an imprecise shape, gardenias are a quick flower to make and a nice option if you don't want to use a rose.

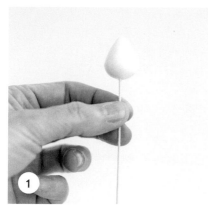

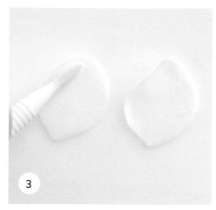

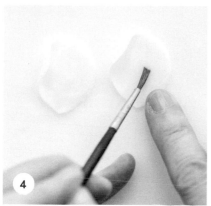

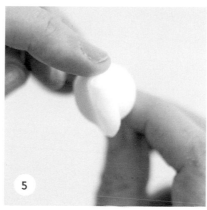

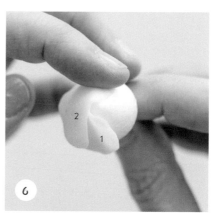

SPECIFICS YOU WILL NEED

···

- White paste
- Moss green paste
- CelBud 2, ¾in (20mm)
- Gardenia petal cutters: rose petal cutters in three sizes, ⅞ x 1in (2.3 x 2.5cm), 1⅛ x 1⅜in (3 x 3.5cm), 1⅜ x 1⅝in (3.5 x 4.3cm)
- Petal veiner (XL rose, Marcel Veldbloem Flower Veiners)
- Gardenia leaf cutter (Sugar Art Studio)
- Gardenia leaf veiner (First Impressions Molds)
- 20g white wire
- 28g green wire
- Dresden tool
- Acoustic "bumpy" foam and foam/tissue bits
- Moss Green and Holly petal dusts
- Confectioner's glaze (optional)

MAKE THE CENTER

1. Glue a CelBud 2 to a 20g white wire. Roll white paste moderately thinly and keep it in a petal protector to prevent it drying.

2. The center is made with six petals together in a spiral. Cut six small petals with the ⅞ x 1in (2.3 x 2.5cm) cutter, and work with two petals at a time. On a foam pad with a ball tool, thin the edges and then lengthen the petals a bit at the tip. Press the petals firmly in the veiner.

3. Working on the front side of the petals on a foam pad, curl the upper left sides of each petal inward with the Dresden tool.

4. Apply sugar glue to the front surface of the petals.

5. Attach the first petal by smoothing the glued side around the cone, positioning the top edge a bit higher than the tip of the CelBud. Leave the curled side open.

6. Attach the second petal by smoothing its glued side over and on top of the first petal, tucking it around the tip of the cone, leaving the curled side slightly open.

7. Prepare two more petals, this time curling the upper left side and along the top edge with the Dresden tool. Apply glue to the right sides.

8. Attach the petals the same way as the first two. Smooth the third petal's glued side over the second petal, leaving the curled side open. And again, the same with the fourth petal. Place the petals high enough so the spiral at the top is covering the tip of the CelBud.

9. Prepare the last two petals, lengthening the tip and stretching them wider before curling the left side and top edges with the Dresden tool. Apply glue on the right sides of the petals.

10. Attach these petals to the flower center, a bit lower this time, smoothing the glued side of the fifth petal over the glued down side of the fourth petal. Repeat with the sixth petal over the fifth petal, leaving the curled sides open.

11. Apply a dab of glue to the base of the first petal and close it over the sixth petal to complete the center. Smooth the bases of all the petals to the cone. Adjust the petals with your fingertips to make them more open or closed as desired. I prefer a less symmetrical look.

MAKE THE MEDIUM PETALS

12. Roll paste moderately thinly and cut six medium 1⅛ x 1⅜in (3 x 3.5cm) petals. On a foam pad with a ball tool, thin the edges and lengthen the center a bit creating a small tip. Press firmly in the veiner.

13. Working on a foam pad, on the front and reverse of the petals, use the Dresden tool to curl random parts of the petal edges including the sides and top edges. Try to make each petal a bit different and mix the curls on the front and reverse sides. Lay the petals in foam or on the back of an apple tray to set for a few minutes until the curls hold their shape.

14. Apply glue to the base of the petals and attach them around the center, making some more closed around the center and leaving some open. Avoid making the spacing too symmetrical by letting some of the petals overlap a bit. Let this layer of petals dry or set firmly before adding the large petals. Use small bits of foam or tissue between the petals to keep them separated.

MAKE THE LARGE PETALS

15. Cut six large 1⅜ x 1⅝in (3.5 x 4.3cm) petals and prepare them in the same way as the medium petals (see steps 12–13). Mix up the curling on the petals to include one side, both sides, top edge or on the reverse. Let some of the petals dry right-side up on the bumpy foam, they will look like they are curling away from the flower.

16. Attach the petals around the flower, layering some of the petals behind the previous layer or slightly offset. Don't use all of the large petals if you don't want them; gaps between petals can look natural and pretty. Let the gardenia dry on foam with tissue or bits of foam between the petals to provide support while drying.

MAKE THE LEAVES

17. Roll moss green paste on a groove board and cut the gardenia leaf shape. Insert a 28g wire ½in (1cm) into the leaf and secure it at the base. Thin the edges of the leaf with a ball tool on a foam pad. Press the leaf in a veiner. Leave to dry on foam.

18. Dust the top of the leaves with a mixture of Moss Green and Holly petal dust and steam to set the color. Finish with a thin layer of confectioner's glaze if desired and leave them to dry before using.

Japanese Anemone

Japanese anemones are the crowning glory of a late summer garden. Growing in pink, lavender or white with bright yellow stamens around a green button center, they can be single or double layered flowers. The shapes of the petals can vary on the same flower, which gives you more leeway in making them. I prefer a lot of stamens around the center, keeping them short and tight so they look full. If you use heavier dusting to deepen the color of the petals, be sure to leave the outer edges untouched to create a pretty outline.

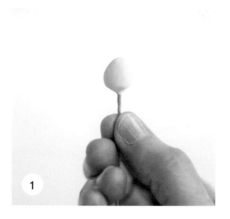

1

2

tip

For a more pollen-heavy look, brush the tips of the dusted stamens with sugar glue and dip the tips in Daffodil "pollen".

3

4

5

SPECIFICS YOU WILL NEED

· Yellow-green paste (Americolor Gels Lemon Yellow + Avocado)
· Pink paste (Wilton Pink)
· Gelatin "pollen" mixture colored with Kiwi and Daffodil petal dust (see Getting Started)
· 22g and 30g white wire
· Yellow-tipped stamens, 60 per flower
· Waxed dental floss
· Floral tape, green and white
· Rose petal cutters: 1⅜ x 1⅝in (3.5 x 4.3cm), or ¾ x 2in (2 x 5cm) for a narrow petal, or 1⅝ x 1¾in (4.3 x 4.5cm) for a rounded petal
· Calyx cutter, 1¼in (3cm), or cutter with sharp pointed tip
· Petal veiner (XL rose, Marcel Veldbloem Flower Veiners)
· Dresden tool
· Apple tray and acoustic "bumpy" foam
· Daffodil, Sunflower, Cosmos, Magenta and Lilac petal dusts

MAKE THE CENTER

1. Roll a ball of yellow-green paste, around ⅜-½in (8-10mm) in size, into a very slight cone shape and attach it to a hooked 22g wire. Gently press on the tip to make it rounded. Allow it to dry completely.

2. Brush the center with sugar glue and roll or dip it in green "pollen" mixture to cover it completely except the underside around the wire. Tap off any excess and allow the center to dry completely.

3. Using a firm brush, dust the tips of about 60 yellow-tipped stamens with a mixture of Daffodil with a bit of Sunflower petal dusts.

4. Secure a length of dental floss to the wire by holding the end of the floss along the wire underneath the center with one hand, and then wrapping the loose end of floss over it four times with your other hand (this prevents having to tie a knot). Using the dental floss, attach a small group of stamens at the base of the center making sure the tips are all sticking out an even distance from underneath the center with minimal filaments showing. Wrap tightly three times with the floss before adding the next group of stamens.

5. Continue adding groups of stamens to surround the center. Trim some of the filaments of the stamens to reduce bulk and then cover the stem by wrapping with white floral tape. If you want more of a pollen-heavy look, see tip.

MAKE THE PETALS

6. Roll pink paste thinly on a groove board, then cut petals with a 1⅜ x 1⅝in (3.5 x 4.3cm) rose petal cutter. Insert a 30g wire ⅖in (1cm) into the groove and secure it at the base. Lengthen the petal centers by ¼–⅖in (5–10mm) on a foam pad with a ball tool.

7. Hold the petal flat and push into the top edge with the tip of a calyx cutter. The indentations should be spaced randomly, and the depths should vary.

8. Press the petal firmly in the veiner.

9. Flip the petal over. On the reverse side, stroke the petal several times down the left and right edges with a Dresden tool to create curled edges. Add a few more ridges on both sides of the wire, coming out from the base of the petal towards the top edge. Make five or six of these petals.

10. Repeat the process for more petals, except this time make them a bit wider by stretching the paste with a ball tool before continuing with the same process. Make five to seven larger petals.

11. For a cupped flower, lay all the petals in an apple tray to dry.

12. For a flower with a mixture of movement, lay some of the petals on the bumps of some acoustic "bumpy" foam so the outer edges bend down and away. Mix these petals with cupped and/or flat petals.

FINISH THE ANEMONE

13. Apply a pale mix of Cosmos and Lilac petal dusts in strokes from the base of the petals upwards and towards the outer edges. Avoid adding color to the outer edges.

14. Using white floral tape, attach the first layer of five or six petals directly under the stamens.

15. Add the second layer of five to seven petals underneath the first as desired.

16. For the narrow petaled variety of anemone, use a narrow cutter, ¾ x 2in (2 x 5cm), and widen the top of each petal a bit with a ball tool before adding the same details with the Dresden tool described in step 9. The flower is made with 15 narrow petals dried face up over bumpy foam and attached in two layers.

17. For the round petaled variety of anemone, use a 1⅝ x 1¾in (4.3 x 4.5cm) rose petal cutter and only use the Dresden tool along the top edge of the reverse side. The flower is made with five petals dried in an apple tray and attached in one layer, or seven to eight petals attached in two layers.

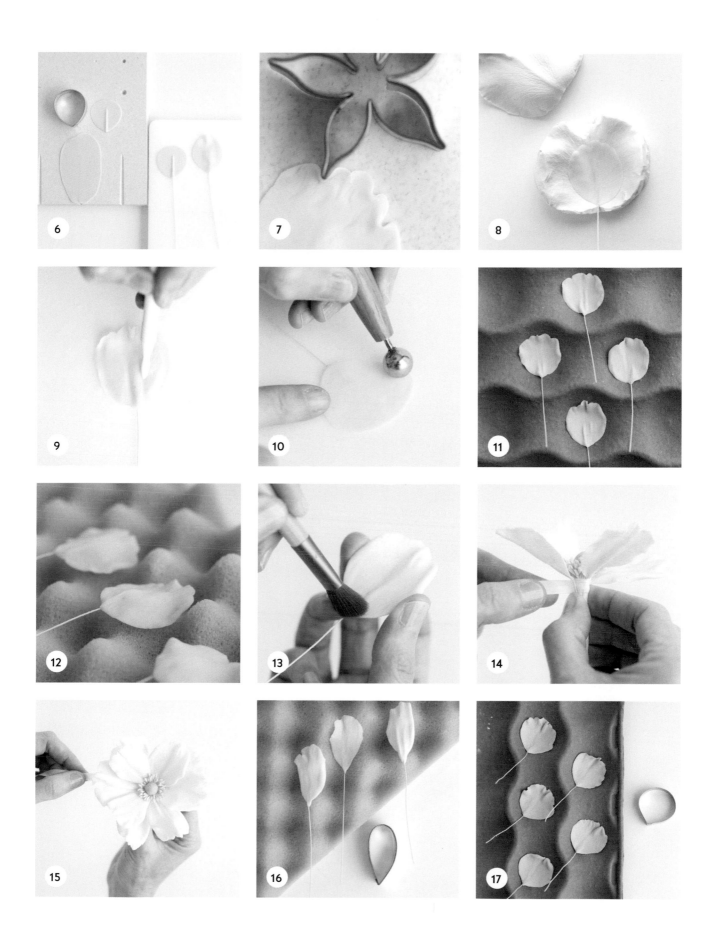

Peony

Peonies are garden classics, loved throughout the world for their extravagant early summer blossoms. Alone or used in mixed arrangements, they have an elegant beauty and are a long-standing favorite for weddings. This version is simply made with layers of petals built up around a styrofoam ball. The quick trick is making each petal a bit unique by pressing and cutting into the top edge with a sharp cutter. The outlined layers are simply a guideline to get started; play around with the number and placement of petals to find a shape and the fullness you love!

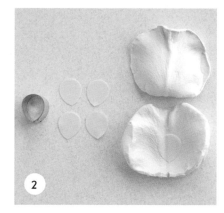

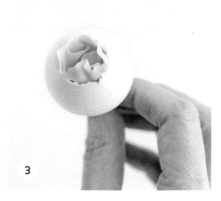

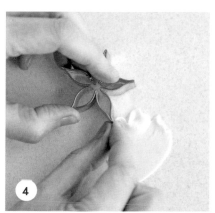

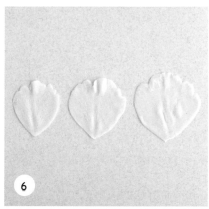

SPECIFICS YOU WILL NEED

· ·

- Pale pink paste (Wilton Pink)
- 18g wire
- 30g wire
- 1½in (4cm) styrofoam ball
- Craft knife
- Rose petal cutters in seven sizes: ¾ x ⅞in (2 x 2.3cm), ⅞ x 1in (2.2 x 2.5cm), 1⅜ x 1⅝in (3.5 x 4.3cm), 2 x 2in (5 x 5cm), 2⅛ x 2¼in (5.4 x 5.5cm), 2 x 2⅜in (5 x 6cm), 1⅞ x 2⅛in (4.7 x 5.4cm)
- Petal veiner (XL rose, Marcel Veldbloem Flower Veiners)
- Dresden tool
- Calyx cutter, 1¾in (4.5cm) or any cutter with a sharp pointed tip
- 1½in (4cm) and 2in (5cm) styrofoam balls for petal formers
- Apple tray for petal former
- Floral tape, white or green
- Pink petal dust

PREPARE THE CENTER

1. Glue a 1½in (4cm) styrofoam ball to an 18g wire. Cut off a ¾in (2cm) width slice off the top with a craft knife. Cut around the circle with a craft knife and hollow out an opening in the ball about ½in (1cm) deep.

2. Roll pale pink paste thinly and cut five ¾ x ⅞in (2 x 2.3cm) rose petals. Press all the petals in a veiner. On a foam pad with a ball tool, lightly ruffle the top edges.

3. Apply sugar glue to the base of the petals on the front and reverse. Fill the opening with the petals, positioning them so they look scrunched together. The top edges of the petals can be a bit above the edge of the opening.

MAKE THE PETALS

4. All the peony petals will be created the same way, but shaped and attached a bit differently. Roll the paste thinly and cut the designated petal shape. On a foam pad with a ball tool, thin the edges. On a firm surface, use the point of a 1¾in (4.5cm) calyx cutter to cut into and press into the top edge of each petal, making it uneven and ragged.

5. Press the petal firmly in the veiner to flatten and thin the petal edges.

6. Make each petal a bit different when cutting and pressing into the top edges.

PETAL LAYER 1

7. Make five ⅞ x 1in (2.3 x 2.5cm) petals following the instructions in steps 4–6.

8. Apply glue to the petals and attach them so they lay flat around the opening. Use them to cover the edge and prevent any of the styrofoam from showing.

PETAL LAYER 2

9. Make five 1⅜ x 1⅝in (3.5 x 4.3cm) petals following the instructions in steps 4–6. Gently stretch and smooth the petals on 1½in (4cm) styrofoam balls so they conform to the shape of the balls. Leave to set long enough to hold their shape.

10. Apply glue to the base and along the sides of the petals and apply in two layers – two petals opposite each other and then petals around.

PETAL LAYER 3

11. Make five 2 x 2in (5 x 5cm) petals following the instructions in steps 4–6. Gently stretch and smooth the petals on 2in (5cm) styrofoam balls. Pinch the paste together at the base and fold over the flap to tighten the petal to the ball.

12. Apply glue to the petals and attach four of them around the center randomly, a bit higher than the previous layer. Attach the fifth petal slightly sideways and open to give the center a bit of asymmetry. This sideways petal will be in a "12 o'clock" position to help with positioning of the outer layers. Let the center dry for at least an hour before adding more layers.

PETAL LAYER 4

13. Make five 2⅛ x 2¼in (5.4 x 5.5cm) petals following the instructions in steps 4–6. Gently stretch and smooth the entire petal on each 2in (5cm) ball; do not pinch the base. This time lift some of the top edges of the petals with a tool or your fingertips.

14. Apply glue to the base of the petals. Attach the first petal over the sideways petal, matching the angle.

15. With the sideways petals at the "12 o'clock" position, attach the next two petals a bit higher than the previous layer at "8 o'clock" and then at "7 o'clock" positions.

16. Apply the remaining two petals at "3 o'clock" and then "4 o'clock" positions. Let this stage of the flower dry for at least an hour.

PETAL LAYER 5 (TRANSITIONAL)

17. These are the transition petals – you can apply them as open or closed as desired. Make seven 2 x 2⅜in (5 x 6cm) petals following the instructions in steps 4–6.

18. With a ball tool on a foam pad, cup in a few spots along the top edge of the petal.

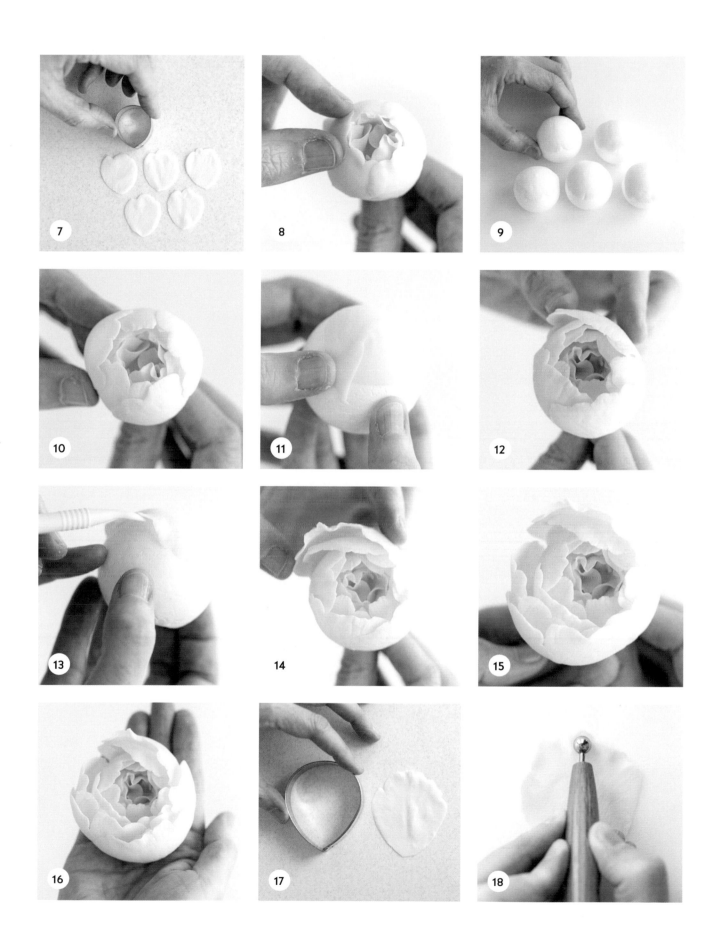

19. Lay the petals in a cupped former or apple tray until they are set and holding their shape. Do not let them dry completely.

20. Apply glue to the base of the petals. With the sideways petals at "12 o'clock", attach three of the petals ¼in (5mm) lower on the flower and a bit open in "half past 11", "half past 12" and "3 o'clock" positions.

21. Attach two more of the petals; one in an "8 o'clock" position, and then the second a bit lower on the flower at "half past 8".

22. Attach the remaining two petals; one at "5 o'clock", and then the second a bit lower in a "4 o'clock" position. Place some foam or bits of tissue between the layers as needed to keep them open. Let the peony dry. Additional non-wired petals may be added as desired.

PETAL LAYER 6

23. For the wired petals, roll the paste thinly on a groove board and cut two sizes of petal: 1⅞ x 2⅛in (4.7 x 5.4cm) and 2 x 2⅜in (5 x 6cm). Insert a 30g white wire ½in (1cm) into each petal and secure at the base.

24. With the calyx cutter, press a few indentations into the top edge and/or cut a few narrow slits. Press the petals in the veiner.

25. Using the Dresden tool on a foam pad, curl some sections along the top edges working on the front and also the back of the petals.

26. Lay some of the petals in an apple tray for a lightly cupped shape. Leave them to dry.

27. Lay some of the petals on the back of the apple tray so they curve gently downwards. Leave them to dry. Make about ten petals depending on the fullness of flower you desire.

28. Using floral tape, attach the cupped petals under the base of the flower, spacing and layering them while trying to avoid a symmetrical shape.

29. Attach the petals that are shaped to curve downwards. Don't be afraid to layer them behind each other for fullness and to avoid too much symmetry. I like to place them on the flower where they will hang over a cake edge or fill a gap between other flowers.

30. With a soft round brush, apply some Pink petal dust in the center of the peony. Steam to set the color and leave it to dry before using

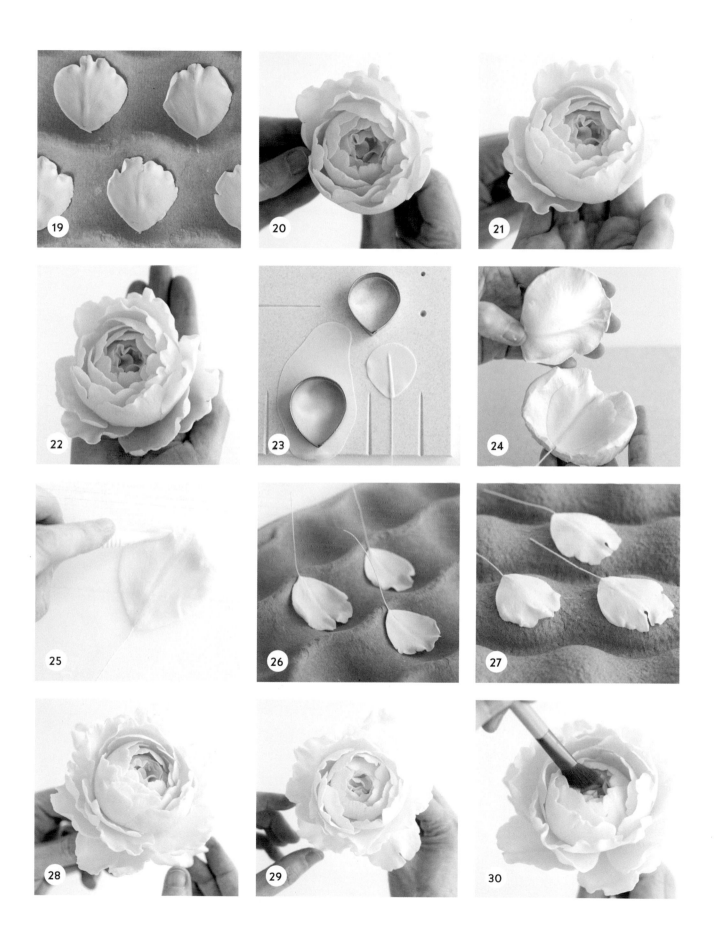

Icelandic Poppy

The poppy provides showy blossoms in late spring to early summer with large bowl-shaped tissue-paper flowers in beautiful bright and sherbet colors. No need for perfect petals here, have fun with the scrunching techniques to create petals that look a bit crushed and crinkled. Use cupped petals only for a flower that is more uniform in shape, and then a mix of cupped and open petals for an over-bloomed stunner.

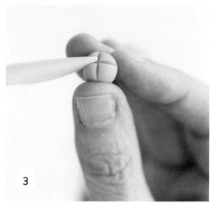

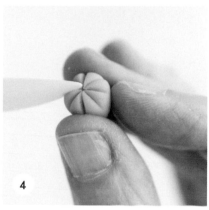

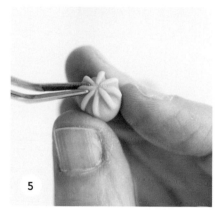

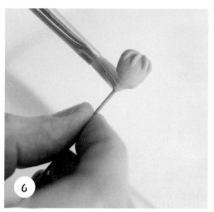

SPECIFICS YOU WILL NEED

- Moss green paste (Wilton Moss Green)
- Pale peach paste (Wilton Creamy Peach or Americolor Gel Copper + a bit of Lemon Yellow)
- 22g green wire
- 28g white wire
- Knife tool
- Tweezers
- Yellow gelatin "pollen" mixture (see Getting Started)
- Waxed dental floss
- Stamens, long head, pointed or hammerhead
- Floral tape, white and green
- Poppy petal cutters: 2 x 2⅜in (5 x 6cm) and 2¼ x 2⅝in (5.5 x 6.7cm) (rose petal cutters, World of Sugar Art or Squires Kitchen)
- Poppy veiner (Sugar Art Studio peony veiner)
- 2½in (6.5cm) half sphere former
- Acoustic "bumpy" foam
- Moss Green, Kiwi, Peach, Daffodil and Cosmos petal dusts

MAKE THE CENTER

1. Roll a ⅜in (8mm) ball of pale moss green paste into a smooth ball.

2. Attach the ball to a hooked 22g wire and secure it at the base.

3. Mark the top of the ball into quarters with a knife tool or a craft knife.

4. Divide each of the quarters in half making eight even sections.

5. Pinch each section with tweezers and then gently smooth the sections with your fingers to make them even. Leave to dry completely.

6. Dust the center with Moss Green petal dust.

7. Carefully apply sugar glue to the pinched sections and then dip them in yellow pollen mixture. Use a firm dry paintbrush to remove any pollen mixture from between the sections.

8. Attach a piece of waxed dental floss to the wire by holding the end underneath the poppy center and wrapping over it with a bit of the floss. This will anchor the floss to the wire without the need for tying a knot.

9. Attach a small bunch of stamens to the center, with the heads sitting a bit above the poppy center. You want to see a bit of the filaments showing when you look at the center from the top. Wrap the floss around tightly three times.

10. Keep adding groups of stamens in the same way, described in step 9, until the center is full.

11. Thin out the filaments with scissors and cover the stem completely with white floral tape.

12. Dust the stamens with Daffodil petal dust.

13. Dab sugar glue on the stamen tips and dip them in the yellow pollen mixture.

14. With a small flat brush, add some Kiwi dust on the filaments at the base of the center.

MAKE THE PETALS

15. Roll pale peach paste thinly on the groove board and cut the petal shapes. Use a mix of two sizes: 2 x 2⅜in (5 x 6cm) and 2¼ x 2⅝in (5.5 x 6.7cm) or all of one of these sizes to make a smaller or larger poppy respectively.

16. Insert 28g white wire ½in (1cm) into each petal. Secure at the base.

17. With a ball tool on a foam pad, gently widen the petals a bit to the left and right.

18. Press each of the wired petals in the veiner.

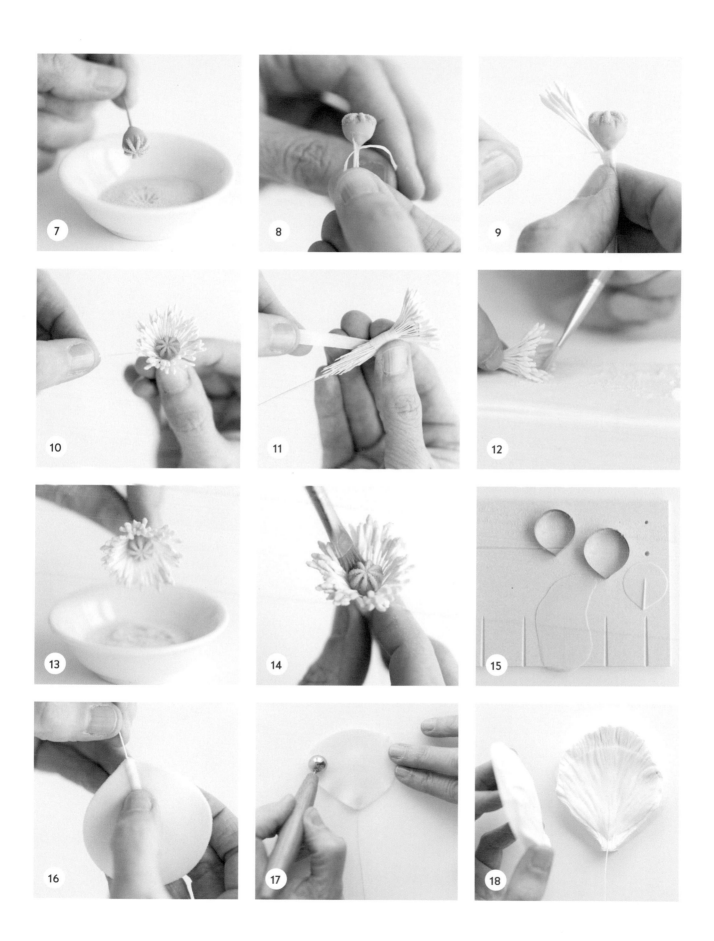

19. With a ball tool on a foam pad, thin and ruffle the most outer edges.

20. Use a Dresden tool to create additional grooves in the petal, making strokes from the outer edge inward.

21. Create a few folds and fold overs with your fingers by scrunching the paste together like tissue paper. Open the petal but leave a few of the folds intact. These should follow the lines of the veining.

22. Additionally scrunch a few small sections of the outer petal edge.

23. For cupped petals, set them into a 2½in (6.5cm) plastic half sphere former with the wires going through a small hole at the bottom of the former. Some of the top petal edges can be curled forwards or backwards with your fingers.

24. For the outer open petals, lay them on "bumpy" foam to dry. Lay some facing up so they have a bit of a cupped base.

25. Lay some tented over the bumps of the foam, encouraging the petal edges to drop down. These will be the over-bloomed outer petals. Make a mix of four to six cupped petals and three to five open petals per flower depending on the size desired.

FINISH THE FLOWER

26. Using a flat brush, dust a mixture of Peach, Daffodil and Cosmos petal dusts from the outer edge of the petal inwards. If desired, add some of the same color to the base of the petals.

27. Using half-width green floral tape, attach the first petal at the base of the stamens.

28. Add two to four more cupped petals, layering a few of them behind others. Avoid making this inner layer too symmetrical or evenly spaced.

29. Add three to five outer petals directly under the first layer. Again, avoid even spacing and let the outer petals overlap a bit.

30. Use all cupped petals for a more uniform poppy shape as shown with the ivory flower pictured.

Heirloom Rose

Known for their large beautiful blooms and amazing fragrance, heirloom roses are technically those that existed before 1867 and the emerging era of rose hybrids. But old is new again, and the vintage-like qualities of heirloom roses are making a comeback! Sturdy enough to stand on their own, they also look amazing mixed with smaller flowers and lots of gorgeous greenery. This beauty has four layers of petals, but don't hesitate to add a few more at the last stage to add depth and fullness to your finished rose.

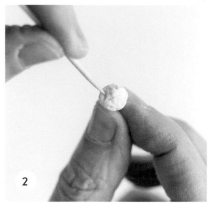

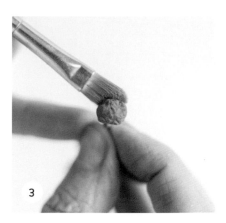

SPECIFICS YOU WILL NEED

- Pale green paste (Americolor Gel Avocado)
- Ivory paste (Americolor Gel Ivory)
- Rose petal cutters in four sizes: 1⅛ x 1⅜in (3 x 3.5cm), 1⅝ x 1¾in (4.3 x 4.5cm), 1½ x 1⅞in (4 x 4.7cm) and 1⅞ x 2⅛in (4.7 x 5.4cm) (World of Sugar Art, Squires Kitchen or other brand)
- Rose petal veiner (XL rose, Marcel Veldbloem Flower Veiners)
- Dresden tool
- 22g, 28g and 30g white wire
- Stamens, 30–40 per flower, rounded, flat or folded tip
- Floral tape, white or green
- 2in (5cm) half sphere former
- 1½in (4cm) half sphere former
- Daffodil, Sunflower, Chestnut, Chocolate Brown, Cosmos, Pink and Cream petal dusts

MAKE THE ROSE CENTER

1. Roll a ⅜in (8mm) ball of pale green paste into a teardrop shape and attach it to a 22g hooked white wire.

2. With the flattened end of a wooden skewer or toothpick (cocktail stick), make rough indentations all over the top. Leave to dry.

3. Dust the center with a mix of Daffodil and Chestnut.

4. Fold the stamens in half. Dust the filaments and tips of the stamens with a mixture of Daffodil and a small amount of Sunflower and Chestnut.

5. Using floral tape, attach several groups of stamens around the center so the stamen heads are ¼–½in (5mm–10mm) higher than the center. Open the stamens with your fingers.

6. Steam to set the dust colors and leave to dry. Dab Chocolate Brown dust mixed with alcohol on some of the stamen head tips and leave to dry.

MAKE THE EXTRA SMALL PETALS

7. Use the four sizes of rose petal cutters to make the various petals, starting with the smallest.

8. Roll ivory colored paste thinly on a groove board and cut a 1⅛ x 1⅜in (3 x 3.5cm) petal. Insert a 30g white wire ½in (1cm) into the petal and secure at the base.

9. On a foam pad with a ball tool, thin the petal edges. Stroke the paste to stretch the petal a little and add some irregularity to the top edge.

10. Press the petal in a veiner.

11. On a foam pad, curl in along the top edge with a Dresden tool.

12. Lay the petal in a 2in (5cm) half sphere former to dry, curling over top edges towards the center. Leave to dry. Make two to three petals.

MAKE THE SMALL PETALS

13. Repeat the process described in steps 8–12, with a 1⅝ x 1¾in (4.3 x 4.5cm) petal cutter. Leave to dry. Make three or four petals.

MAKE THE MEDIUM PETALS

14. Roll more paste and cut a 1½ x 1⅞in (4 x 4.7cm) petal. Insert a 30g white wire and secure it at the base. Press the petal in the veiner.

15. This time lay the petal face down on a foam pad. Use a Dresden tool to curl the top edge of the petal towards you so it will end up curling backwards on the finished petal.

16. Feed the wire down through a hole in the 2in (5cm) former, smoothing the front of the petal to conform to the former. Let the top edge of the petal curl backwards over the top of the former.

17. To prevent the curls from collapsing, slide a paintbrush or wooden skewer underneath until they are set. Leave to dry. Make five or six of these petals.

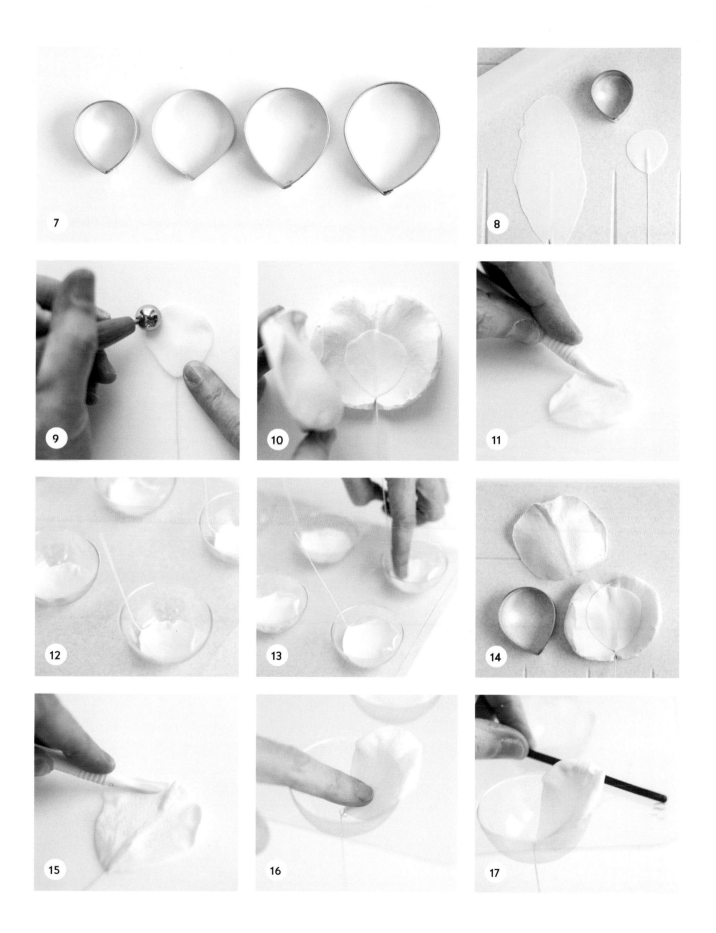

MAKE THE LARGE PETALS

18. Using 28g white wire and a 1⅞ x 2⅛in (4.7 x 5.4cm) cutter, repeat the same process of making and wiring petals described in steps 8–10.

19. Lay the petals face down on a foam pad. Use a Dresden tool to curl the top edge and a third of the way down the outer edges of the petals towards you so that they will end up curling backwards on the finished petals.

20. Curl some of the petals heavily so the top edges almost come to a point, as shown.

21. Feed the wires down through a hole in the 1½in (4cm) former and smooth the front of the petals so they conform to the former. Let the top two thirds of the petal lay out on the flat surface of the former. Leave to dry. Make five or six petals.

DUST THE PETALS

22. Dust the base of the petals with pale Daffodil petal dust.

23. Dust the edges of the petals with a mixture of Cosmos, Pink and Cream. Draw the color from the outer edges inward but leave the middle of the petals the ivory color of the paste.

24. Group your petals by size for quicker assembly.

ASSEMBLE THE ROSE

25. Using white floral tape, attach the extra small petals at the base of the stamens.

26. Add the small petals directly underneath and around the extra small petals.

27. Add five or six medium petals, letting some overlap to avoid too much symmetry.

28. Add the large petals, again letting some overlap to avoid an overly symmetrical arrangement. Space or a gap between petals can look more natural. Tape all the way down over the wires to create a single stem. Steam the flower to set the dust colors and leave to dry.

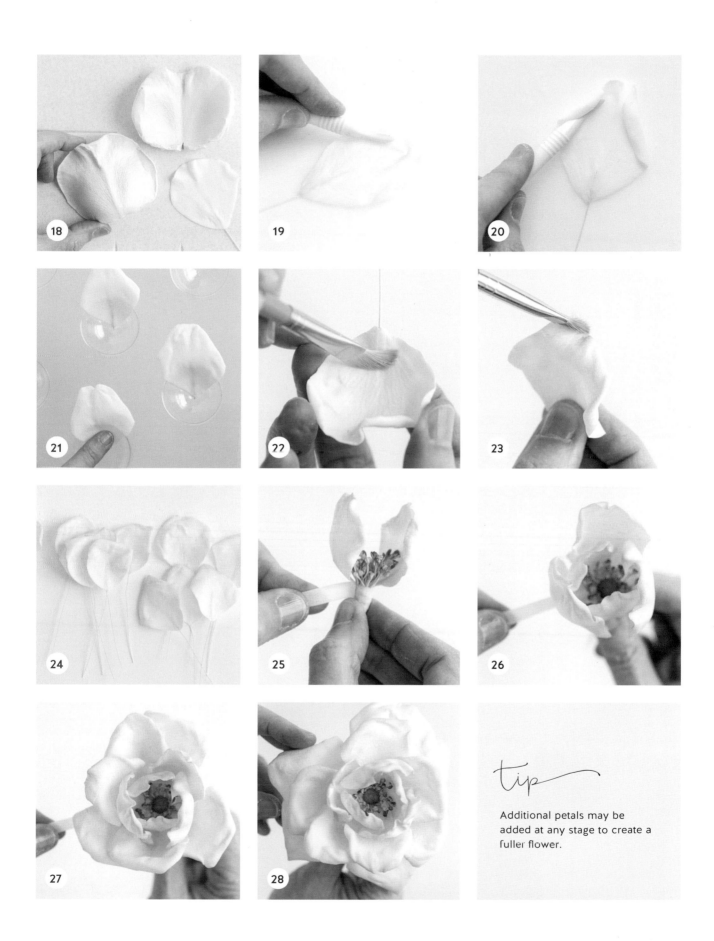

tip

Additional petals may be added at any stage to create a fuller flower.

Heritage Rose

Charming and perfectly cup-shaped, this rose is made with a center that is busy with petals, surrounded by delicate outer layers that curl back just a bit. English-style roses can be time consuming to create, so I reduced the number of inner petal "sets" to three, and had some fun layering the individual petals unevenly (on purpose!) to create a more relaxed and organic feel to the finished rose. You can easily add more petal "sets" or single petals to fill the center as you wish.

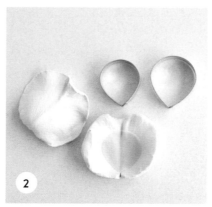

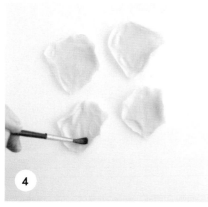

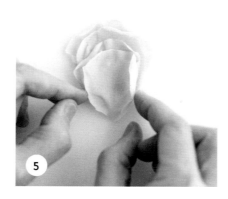

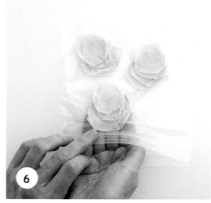

SPECIFICS YOU WILL NEED

···

- Pale pink paste (Wilton Pink)
- White paste (optional)
- Moss green paste (for calyx) (Wilton Moss Green + Americolor Gel Lemon Yellow)
- Rose petal cutters in three sizes: 1⅜ x 1⅝in (3.5 x 4.3cm), 1⅝ x 1⅞in (4.3 x 4.7cm) and 1⅞ x 2⅛in (4.7 x 5.4cm)
- 2½–3in (6.5–7.5cm) calyx cutter (any brand)
- Rose petal veiner (XL rose, Marcel Veldbloem Flower Veiners)
- 18g white or green wire
- 1½in (4cm) styrofoam ball
- 1½in (4cm) circle cutter
- 2in (5cm) and 2⅜in (6cm) styrofoam balls (for petal formers)
- Dresden tool
- Plastic zip-top bag or small airtight container
- Kiwi, Moss Green and Magenta petal dusts for calyx

MAKE THE BASE

1. Cut a 1½in (4cm) styrofoam ball in half and glue an 18g wire into the base. Roll pale pink paste very thinly and cut a 1½in (4cm) circle. Apply sugar glue to the circle of paste and attach it to the flat surface of the ball.

MAKE THE INNER PETALS

2. Roll pale pink paste thinly and place it in a petal protector to prevent drying. All the inner petals will be created the same way. Cut six 1⅜ x 1⅝in (3.5 x 4.3cm) rose petals and six 1⅝ x 1⅞in (4.3 x 4.7cm) rose petals. Thin the edges on a foam pad with a ball tool and press in a petal veiner. Keep the petals covered to prevent drying.

3. Work with four petals at a time, two of the smaller and two of the larger petals. Using a Dresden tool on a foam pad, tightly curl in bits of the outer edges all around each petal.

4. Lay out the four petals and brush glue to cover the bottom third of the petals. Do not put glue over the entire surface, you don't want them to become a solid mass.

5. Layer the petals on top of each other into a "set" consisting of the two large petals on the bottom topped with the two smaller petals. Don't center the petals perfectly on top of each other, let some of the edges overlap and be mismatched, and vary the heights too. Lay the set flat into a plastic bag or tightly sealed container to prevent them drying out while you make two more sets.

6. Repeat with the remaining petals so you have three sets.

7. To finish the sets, dab glue on the bottom third across the set. Gently roll the right side of the set to the middle and fold the left side over it. Press gently, avoiding squishing and flattening the base of the set.

8. Glue and roll the remaining two sets of petals.

9. Using small scissors, trim ¼in (5mm) off the bottom of two sets and ½in (1cm) off the third. This will give the sets a slightly varied height.

10. Apply glue to the flat surface of the ball.

11. Place the first set near the edge of the flat surface of the ball. Gently bend it towards the center while pressing it to the flat surface.

12. Attach the second set in the same way. Dab glue on the outside of the outer petals of the two sets to help them stick together. Try not to scrunch and squeeze the sets together tightly.

13. Attach the third set into the remaining space. Dab glue on the outside of the outer petals in between the sets to help them stick together.

14. Allowing a small gap between the sets is natural looking, but if you don't care for it you can fill any spaces with single petals that are curled on the edges and then folded and trimmed to fit.

15. Use a Dresden tool to separate and open the petals so they are not too condensed. Pinch some of the outer petals to make them look a little bit creased.

MAKE THE SUPPORT PETALS

16. Roll paste thinly and cut five 1⅜ x 1⅝in (3.5 x 4.3cm) rose petals. Thin the edges with a ball tool and press them in the veiner. One at a time, smooth the petals over 2in (5cm) styrofoam balls until they conform to the balls. Let them set until they firmly hold their shape.

17. Apply glue along the sides and at the base of the petals. Attach them evenly spaced around the halved 1½in (4cm) styrofoam ball with the top edges of the petals sitting below the curled top edges of the petal sets. Leave to dry for at least an hour before proceeding with the outer petals.

MAKE THE OUTER PETALS

18. For layer one: roll the paste thinly and place it in a petal protector to prevent drying. Cut six 1⅝ x 1⅞in (4.3 x 4.7cm) rose petals, thin the edges with a ball tool on a foam pad and press firmly in the petal veiner.

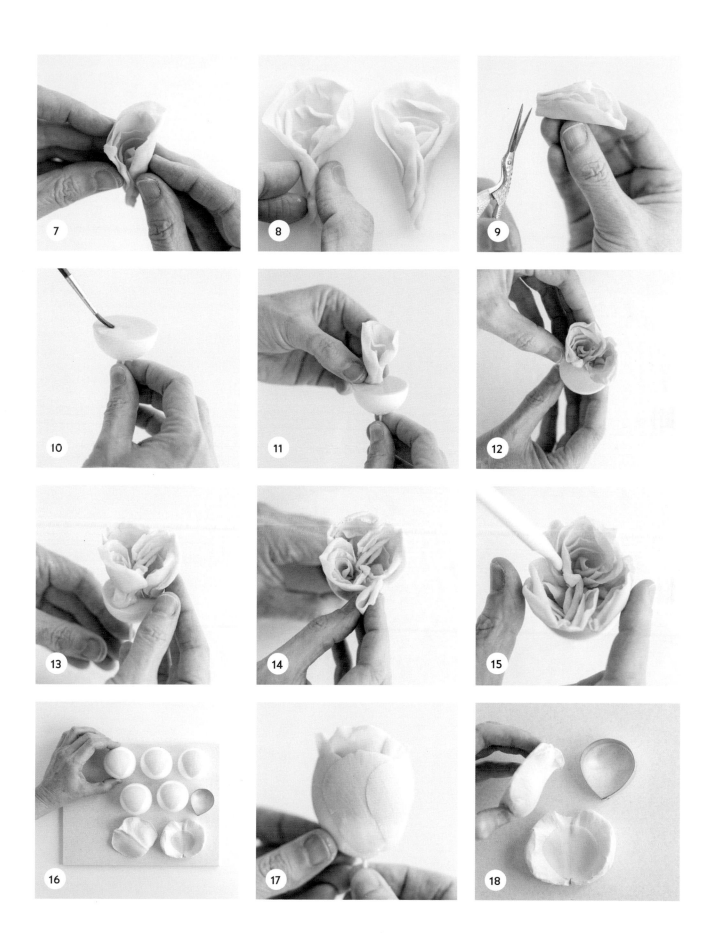

19. One at a time, smooth the petals face down over the 2in (5cm) styrofoam balls until they conform to the shape of the balls. Let the petals set until they hold their shape well but are not completely dry.

20. When the petals are holding their shape, apply glue on the inside edge in a v-shape down the outer edges to the point of the petal.

21. Attach the first petal to the halved 1½in (4cm) styrofoam ball so the top edge sits at or just above the top edge of the support petals.

22. Add the remaining five petals evenly spaced around the center, tucking the last petal into the first. Gently open the petals so there is a ⅛in (3mm) gap between the support petals and the first outer layer.

23. For layer two: using a 1⅞ x 2⅛in (4.7 x 5.4cm) rose petal cutter, make five more cupped petals on 2⅜in (6cm) styrofoam balls in the same way as you did in step 19. This time gently lift sections of the top edges with a Dresden tool to give the petals some wavy movement or soft curled back edges. Let them set until they hold their shape.

24. Attach these petals evenly spaced around the flower at the same height as the previous layer, tucking the last petal into the first. Allow this layer to be a bit more open at the top. You can finish the rose at this step with a calyx or add the last layer of curled open petals in the next step.

25. For layer three (final layer): make between three and five more 1⅞ x 2⅛in (4.7 x 5.4cm) petals. As you smooth them on to 2⅜in (6cm) styrofoam balls, curl back larger sections of the top edges with your fingertips.

26. Prop up the styrofoam balls in small cutters to prevent the curled edges of the petals from collapsing while they are setting.

27. Attach the petals, sitting them lower on the flower and spacing them as desired. Let the rose dry completely.

ADD THE CALYX (OPTIONAL)

28. Roll moss green paste moderately thinly and cut a 2½– 3in (6.5–7.5cm) calyx shape. Thin the edges and stretch the calyx with a ball tool on a foam pad. Use small scissors to snip feathery edges by pointing the scissor tips towards the middle of the calyx.

29. Cup sections of the calyx with the Dresden tool. Apply glue to the center and a bit out on the sections of the calyx. Apply to the base of the flower and leave to dry. Dust with a mixture of Kiwi and Moss Green petal dusts. Add a touch of Magenta on the tips if desired.

DUST THE ROSE

30. If working with pale colors, I prefer to leave the flower as is, or add dust in a very pale version of the paste color in the shadows between the inner petals. If working with dark colored paste, use a small round brush to apply a deeper color in the shadows between the inner petals to add some contrast, as well as some color on the edges of the outer petals. Steam to set the color and let the rose dry before using.

tip

For a natural color variation in a lighter colored rose, make the inner petals one color and then add white to lighten the same paste for the outer petals.

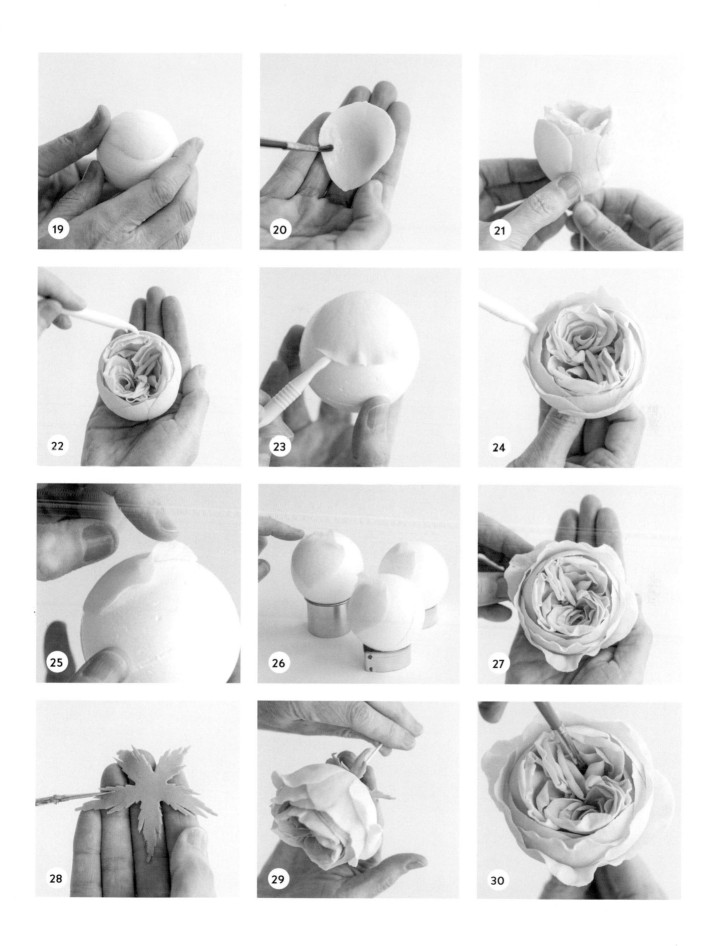

Rose

This rose was inspired by the gorgeous and
popular "reflexed" roses used by florists. The
outer petals of a simple rose are opened and
then flipped and bent backwards, creating lush
layers of petals and turning ordinary roses
into voluminous blooms. This sugar version
is created with a spiraled center and then
finished with delicate petals that are curled
and layered to add beautiful fullness.

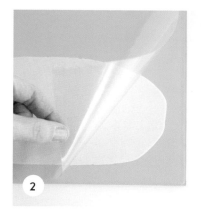

SPECIFICS YOU WILL NEED

- Pale pink paste (Wilton Pink)
- Rose petal cutters in three sizes: 1½ x 1⅞in (4 x 4.7cm), 1⅞ x 2⅛in (4.7 x 5.4cm) and 2 x 2⅜in (5 x 6cm) (World of Sugar Art or Squires Kitchen)
- Rose petal veiner (XL rose, Marcel Veldbloem Flower Veiners)
- 18g white wire
- CelBud 3, 1in (24mm)
- Small paintbrushes (handles used for curling petal edges)
- Foam and tissue
- Acoustic "bumpy" foam
- Cosmos petal dust

MAKE THE ROSE BASE

1. Glue a CelBud 3 to an 18g white wire and set aside.

MAKE THE CENTER

2. The rose center is made with 14 petals. First, roll pale pink paste very thinly. Keep the paste covered in a petal protector to prevent it drying.

3. Cut one 1½ x 1⅞in (4 x 4.7cm) rose petal. Thin the edge with a ball tool on a foam pad.

4. Press in the veiner and then apply sugar glue over the whole petal.

5. Turn the petal lengthwise and attach the center of the petal to the CelBud so the top edge is ¼in (5mm) higher than the tip of the bud.

6. Wrap and smooth the right side of the petal around the bud.

7. Wrap and smooth the left side over, hiding the tip of the bud with a small spiral of paste.

8. Prepare two more petals of the same size in the same way. This time apply glue down the middle and on the right sides of the petals.

9. Attach the middle of both petals on opposite sides of the bud at the same height as the first petal. Smooth the glued sides to the bud.

10. Add a dab of glue to the petal edges that are open, then wrap and smooth them closed on the bud, including at the bottom.

11. Create a second set of the same petals in the same way. Attach the middle of the petals over the edge of petals of the previous layer and smooth the glued sides. Add a bit of glue to the open edges and smooth to close around the bud. Curl back a tiny bit of the top edges of the petals with your fingertips.

12. Create three more petals of the same size in the same way. This time, attach all three evenly around the flower, smoothing the glued sides first. These may be slightly higher than the previous layer.

13. Add a bit of glue to the open sides and then smooth them closed around the bud.

14. Repeat with a second layer of three of the same size petals. Place them slightly higher than the previous layer and use a Dresden tool to open them up a bit.

15. Cut three 1⅞ x 2⅛in (4.7 x 5.4cm) petals and press them in the veiner. Working on the back of the petal, curl along the top edges with a slender paintbrush handle. This will be the outermost layer for the inside of the flower before you make and add the petals peeling away from the center.

16. Apply glue to the right sides of the petals and attach them evenly spaced around the center. Smooth down the glued sides. Then apply glue to the bottom half of the open sides and close them around the bud. These petals should sit higher and be more open than the previous layer.

17. Use your fingertips to encourage the outer edges to curl back.

18. Let the center of the flower dry for about an hour before adding the outer petals.

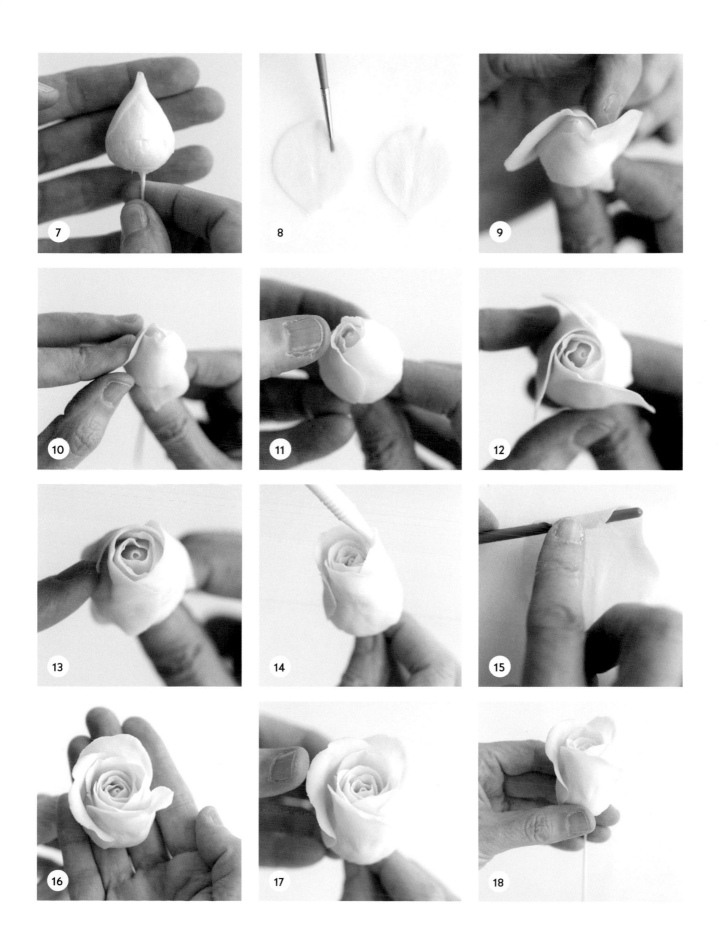

MAKE THE OUTER PETALS

19. Cut three 2 x 2⅜in (5 x 6cm) petals and press them in the veiner. Working on the reverse of the petals, curl back the top left and right edges with a paintbrush handle, creating large curls so the petal tips will come close to or actually to a point. Curl a smaller amount of the bottom left and right edges.

20. The petals should look close to diamond-shaped, as the front and back of the petal pictured show.

21. Lay the petals face up over scrunched up bits of tissue or foam to set, just until they hold their shape. Use your fingers to encourage and shape the curls as needed.

22. Apply glue to the bottom third of the petals and attach the first petal in an "8 o'clock" position.

23. Attach petal two at a "1 o'clock" position and petal three at "4 o'clock".

24. Let these petals set completely before adding additional layers, or the rose will be difficult to handle. Dry with bits of tissue under the outer petals to support them.

25. Make five more of the same size petals in the same way, letting them set just long enough to hold their curled edges.

26. Apply the first three petals in "half past 9", "12 o'clock" and "3 o'clock" positions.

27. Apply the remaining two petals in "7 o'clock" and "half past 5" positions. Additional petals may be added as desired – try not to make the petals too symmetrical.

28. Hang to dry, using small bits of foam or tissue to keep the petal layers separate.

29. Dust only the edges of the petals with pale Cosmos dust and steam to set the color. These beauties look great in both pastels and deep colors. Keep the dusting simple since the petals are fragile.

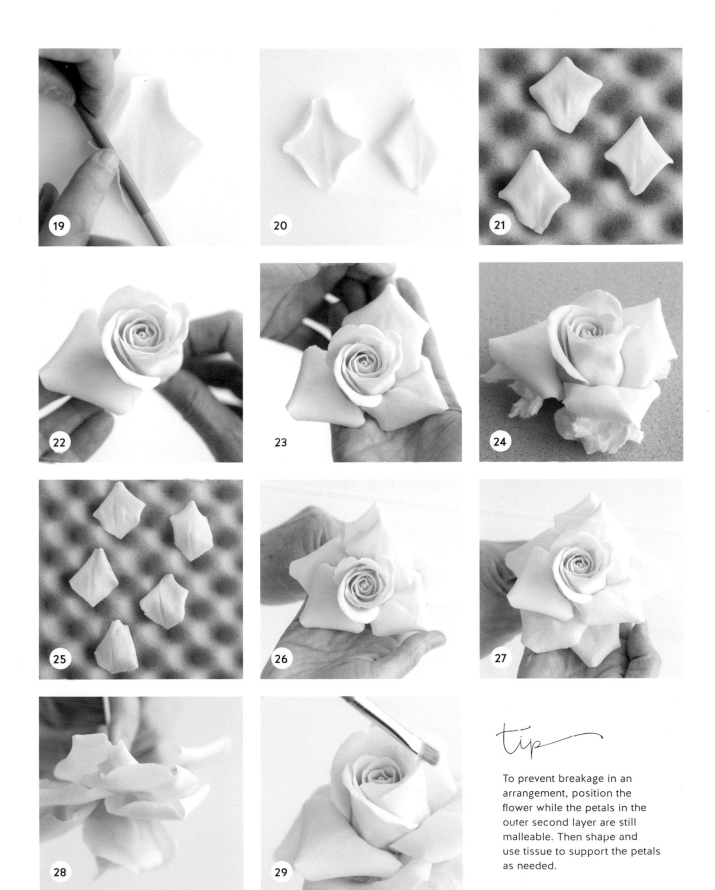

tip

To prevent breakage in an arrangement, position the flower while the petals in the outer second layer are still malleable. Then shape and use tissue to support the petals as needed.

Saucer Magnolia

The goblet-shaped flowers of the saucer magnolia are made up of tepals which can be white, pink or purple with beautiful creamy white interiors. I've made this version using white and pink pastes rolled together, mostly to cut down time in dusting with color. But if you love the dusting part, make the tepals white and have some fun with your pinks! Use a variety of flower sizes for a more natural look in an arrangement, and don't forget to try the sweet magnolia bud too!

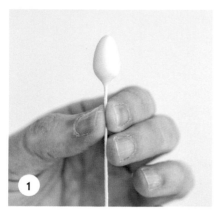

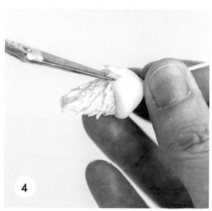

SPECIFICS YOU WILL NEED

....

- Ivory paste (Americolor Gel Ivory)
- White paste
- Pale pink paste (Wilton Pink or Chefmaster Fuchsia)
- Magnolia cutters, set of three: 1¾ x 2⅞in (4.5 x 7.5cm), 1½ x 2¾in (4 x 7cm), 1⅛ x 2½in (3 x 6.5cm) (World of Sugar Art)
- Magnolia veiner (Marcel Veldbloem Flower Veiners)
- 20g, 26g and 28g white wire
- Cutting wheel
- Dresden tool
- Apple tray former
- Floral tape, white (brown or green can be used on the stems if desired)
- CelBud 2, ¾in (20mm), for the bud
- Chestnut, Daffodil, Sunflower, Magenta, Aubergine petal dusts, for the center
- Cosmos, Magenta and Lilac petal dusts, for petals

MAKE THE CENTER

1. Make the flower center in two parts. For the first part, roll a ½in (1cm) ball of ivory paste into a narrow cone shape ¾in (2cm) long. Attach it to a 20g hooked white wire and secure at the base.

2. Use small scissors to cut fine snips around the entire surface except close to the wire. Leave to dry completely before moving on to the second part in step 3.

3. For the second part, dab the bottom quarter of the dried center with sugar glue. Roll a ½in (1cm) ball of ivory paste and slide it up the wire to attach it over the base of the center, shaping it evenly around the base like a tire but with a tapered base, as shown.

4. Using small scissors, snip points where the fresh paste meets the dried center. Make these snips a bit larger than the points created in the first part of the center.

5. Once the inner layer of snips is finished, continue snipping the rest of the paste in the same way but in a slightly larger size, also making the snips a bit more open as you go. Leave the very bottom of the center smooth so the tepals will lay smoothly against it. Leave to dry completely.

6. Dust the top part of the center with a mixture of Chestnut, Sunflower and Daffodil petal dusts.

7. Use a mixture of Magenta petal dust and a tiny bit of Aubergine dust on the lower section, trying to get most of it between the snipped points. Tap off any excess dust, then steam to set the colors and leave the center to dry before using.

MAKE THE LARGE TEPALS

8. Roll white paste on a groove board until almost as thin as desired.

9. Roll pale pink paste over the top and finish rolling to the desired thinness.

10. Cut the large 1¾ x 2⅞in (4.5 x 7.5cm) tepal shape. Insert a 26g white wire up ½in (1cm) into it and secure at the base.

11. Using a cutting-wheel, trim the bulbous outer edges at the base to a wide V-shape.

12. With a ball tool on a foam pad, thin the edges and then press the tepal in the veiner pink side down.

13. On a foam pad, curl the outer edges inward with a Dresden tool.

14. Lay the tepal in an apple tray and leave it to dry. Make six large tepals.

MAKE THE MEDIUM TEPALS

15. Prepare the medium 1½ x 2¾in (4 x 7cm) tepals the same way as the large tepals.

16. Lay the medium tepals in an apple tray and leave them to dry. Make three medium tepals.

MAKE THE SMALL TEPALS

17. Prepare the paste in same way as for the previous tepals, but use 28g white wire for the small 1⅛ x 2½in (3 x 6.5cm) tepals. Curl the edges with the Dresden tool.

18. Let the small tepals dry on "bumpy" foam. This shape will make them look like they are falling away from the bottom of the flower. If you want them softly cupped, dry them in the apple tray like the larger tepals.

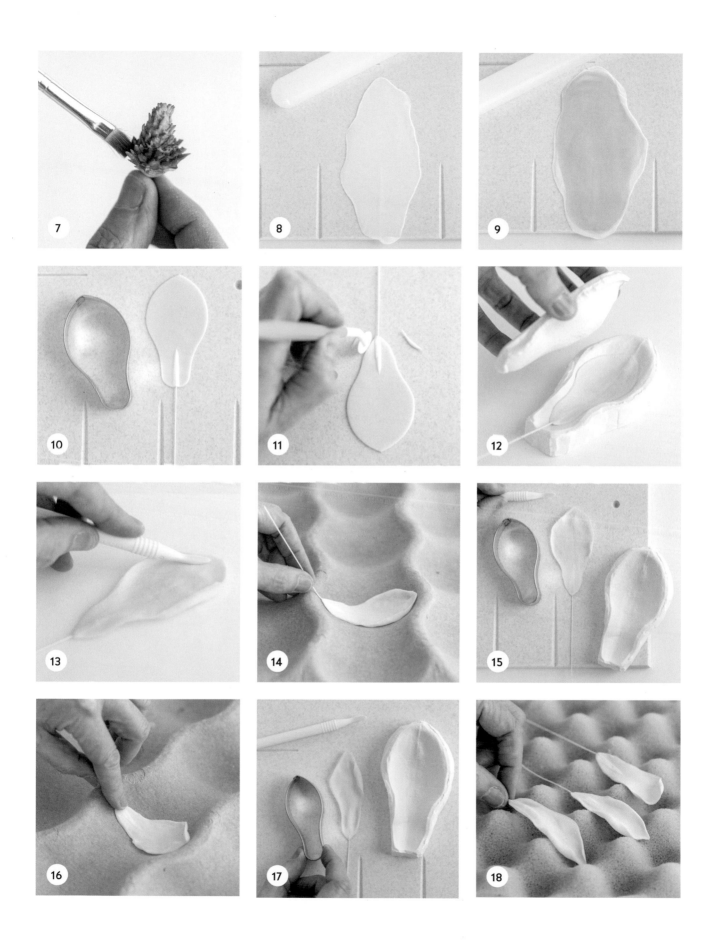

DUST THE TEPALS

19. Use a mix of Cosmos, Magenta and Lilac dusts for the magnolia tepals. Gently dust the reverse side of the tepals from the base upwards, varying the length of your strokes. Some varieties are dark pink, while others are lighter.

ASSEMBLE THE FLOWER

20. Using white floral tape, attach the first large tepal under the base of the flower center.

21. Attach two more large tepals evenly spaced around the center to finish the first layer.

22. Add a second layer of three tepals to fill the gaps between the first set of tepals.

23. Medium and small tepals can be added as desired. For a full flower, add three medium tepals and another three small tepals. Vary the size of your magnolias in an arrangement for a more natural look.

MAKE THE BUD

24. Glue a CelBud 2 onto a 20g white wire.

25. Roll a layer of white and a layer of pale pink pastes together (as you did in steps 8 and 9) and use the medium 1½ x 2¾in (4 x 7cm) cutter for the tepals.

26. On a foam pad with a ball tool, thin the edges and then press the tepals in the veiner pink side down.

27. Curl the outer edges inwards with a Dresden tool.

28. Apply sugar glue to the bottom half of the tepals and on the CelBud. Attach three tepals directly to the CelBud smoothing them to fit tightly to the styrofoam bud to cover and conceal it. Trim any excess paste from the bottom of the bud with scissors.

29. Add more tepals as desired, using bits of tissue to prop them open while the bud hangs to dry.

30. Once dry, leave the bud as is, or carefully dust in the same way as you did for the wired tepals with strokes of pink from the base of the bud upwards. Steam to set the color and leave to dry before using.

tip

You can easily skip the veiner if you don't have one, the curled tepals will still look beautiful. Make sure your paste is rolled thin, and use a ball tool to thin your tepal edges before using the Dresden tool.

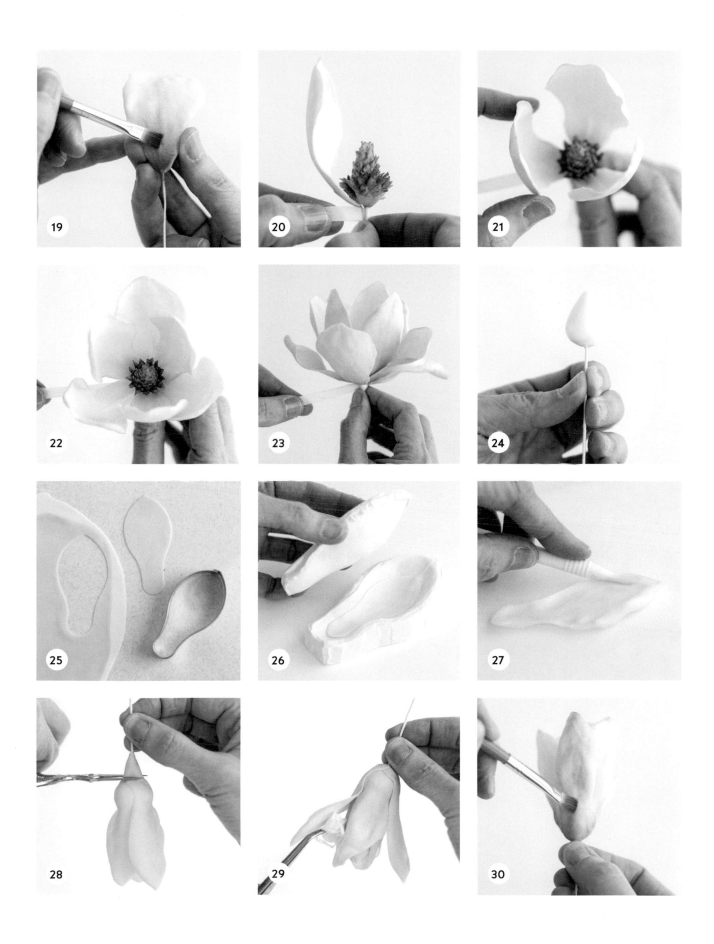

Butterfly Ranunculus

Lithe and elegant, butterfly ranunculus are known for their delicate petals, like butterfly wings. They grow in shades of yellow, pink, orange and ivory, and are the perfect willowy flower to help create a flowing line in an arrangement. For the most natural look, use a mix of petal shapes as outlined below, and don't worry too much about a perfectly symmetrical shape.

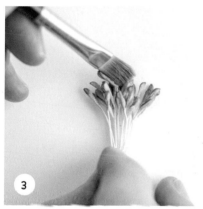

tip

Some butterfly ranunculus varieties have a green center or stamens that are yellow or pale green. With so many beautiful options, use images of real flowers for more inspiration!

SPECIFICS YOU WILL NEED

- Light brown paste (Americolor Gel Warm Brown)
- Yellow paste (Americolor Gel Lemon Yellow)
- Ranunculus cutters: rose petal cutters in three sizes, ⅞ x 1in (2.3 x 2.5cm), 1⅛ x 1⅜in (3 x 3.5cm) and 1⅜ x 1⅝in (3.5 x 4.3cm) (World of Sugar Art), all cutters flattened on the top
- Petal veiner (XL rose, Marcel Veldbloem Flower Veiners)
- 22g and 30g white wire
- Gelatin "pollen" mixture colored with Dark Chocolate Brown petal dust (see Getting Started)
- Stamens, 40–45 per flower, long head or hammerhead
- Donut, Chocolate Brown, Daffodil, Sunflower, Champagne and Pink petal dusts

- Apple tray former
- Waxed dental floss
- Floral tape, white or green

RANUNCULUS BUD

- Yellow green paste (Americolor Gel Avocado + Lemon Yellow, or Sugarflair Gooseberry)
- 1⅜ x 1⅝in (3.5 x 4.3cm) rose petal cutter (World of Sugar Art), flattened on top
- 1¾in (4.5cm) calyx cutter (any brand)
- 24g green wire
- ⅝in (1.5cm) styrofoam ball
- Kiwi petal dust

MAKE THE CENTER

1. Roll a ⅜in (8mm) ball of light brown paste into a teardrop shape with a rounded top. Attach it to a hooked 22g wire. Leave to dry.

2. Dab the center with sugar glue and roll it in dark brown pollen mixture. Leave to dry.

3. Dust the heads of 40–45 stamens with a mixture of Donut and Chocolate Brown petal dust.

4. Using waxed dental floss anchored to the wire, attach small groups of stamens tightly around the center until it is surrounded. Wrap over the floss with white floral tape to secure. Add more dust to the stamens if needed. Steam to set the color and let dry before adding petals.

5. The cutters are rose petal shapes that have been flattened on the top. The sizes are provided in the Specifics You Will Need list. Use any mix of the two larger sizes for most of the petals. Use the smallest cutter only if you want a few petals that are just opening around the center. To create the flat-top shaped cutters, flatten metal rose petal cutters by pressing the top edges gently on a firm surface.

6. Roll pale yellow paste thinly on a groove board and cut a petal. Insert a 30g white wire ½in (1cm) into the petal and secure at the base.

7. With a ball tool on a foam pad, gently stretch the petal to widen and lengthen it a bit and give the top edge some slight irregularity.

8. Press the petal in the veiner.

9. On some of the petals, create a few fine creases and folds vertically down the petal by pinching paste between your two thumbs or scrunching the paste like tissue paper. Open the petal back up but don't smooth out the creases.

10. Lay some of the petals on the top side of an apple tray to dry in both a cupped shape and laying over the ridges. Leave to dry.

11. Lay some of the petals over the reverse side of an apple tray, in both a cupped shape (in the valleys) and on the top of the domes so they curve slightly downwards. Leave the petals to dry.

ASSEMBLE THE RANUNCULUS

12. Using waxed dental floss, attach a first layer of three to six cupped petals directly underneath the stamens, wrapping tightly. Allow space between petals and even overlapping some is more natural than making them evenly spaced around the center.

13. Repeat with a second layer of five to seven petals using a mix of cupped petals and those that have been dried to curve down and away from the base of the flower. Don't be afraid to almost directly overlap petals to create fullness and avoid a symmetrical shape.

14. Wrap green floral tape over the floss and all the way down the wires to create a single stem. Steam gently to set the dust colors. The flowers are more natural-looking when they are made with a mix of cupped and open petals as shown.

DUST THE RANUNCULUS

15. Dust the outer edges of the petals with a mixture of Daffodil and a tiny bit of pale Sunflower petal dusts.

16. Add a touch of the Daffodil at the base of the petals to deepen the color of the center of the flower. Steam to set the dust colors and leave to dry.

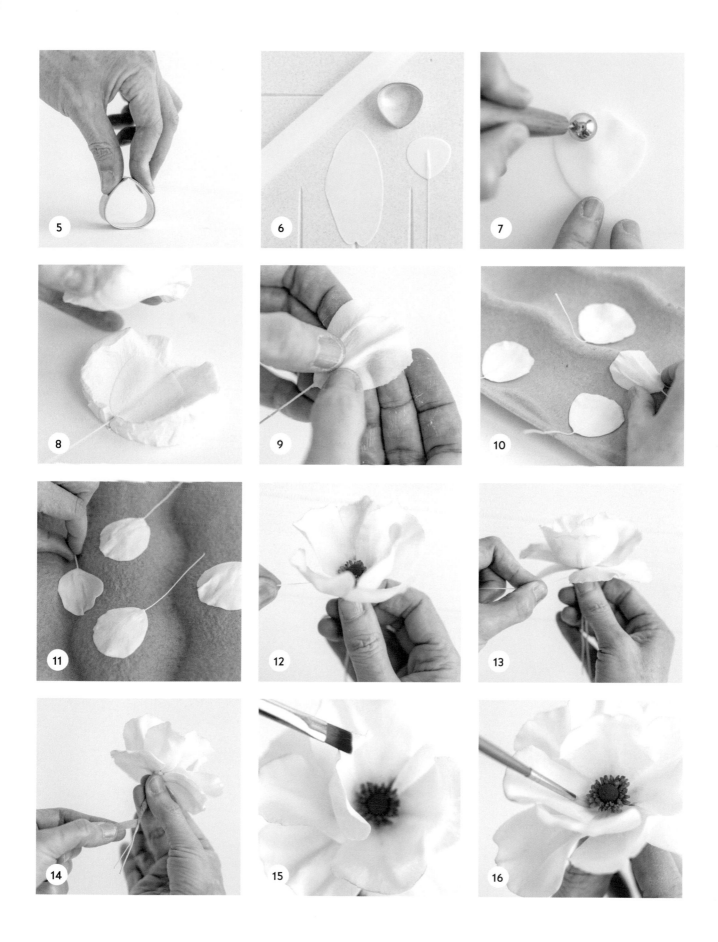

17. Additional varieties include white and various shades of pink.

18. This ranunculus is also pretty with ivory colored petals and dusty pink around the center. Dust the petal edges with Champagne, and around the center with Pink.

MAKE THE RANUNCULUS BUD

19. Glue a ⅝in (1.5cm) styrofoam ball to a 24g green wire.

20. Roll pale yellow paste thinly and keep it in a petal protector to prevent it from drying. Cut five 1½ x 1⅝in (4 x 4.3cm) petals.

21. Press the petals in the veiner and then gently pinch vertically down the petals to create a few fine creases.

22. Apply glue to the base of all the petals and on the ball.

23. Attach three of the petals to the ball, then gently scrunch them so they close over the top of the ball to hide it.

24. Apply the remaining two petals, smoothing them on to the first layer, but letting them be more open. Additional petals may be added if a fuller bud is desired. Hang to dry.

25. Roll yellow-green paste thinly and cut a 1¾in (4.5cm) calyx shape.

26. With a ball tool on a foam pad, thin the edges. Using a Dresden tool, stroke down both sides of the sections firmly to cup them.

27. Apply glue and attach to the base of the bud, slightly overlapping some of the sections to make the calyx look more natural. Leave to dry.

28. Dust Kiwi petal dust on the calyx sections and up on to the base of the bud. Apply Daffodil dust in the folds of the paste from the base of the bud upwards. Steam to set the dust colors and leave the bud to dry before using.

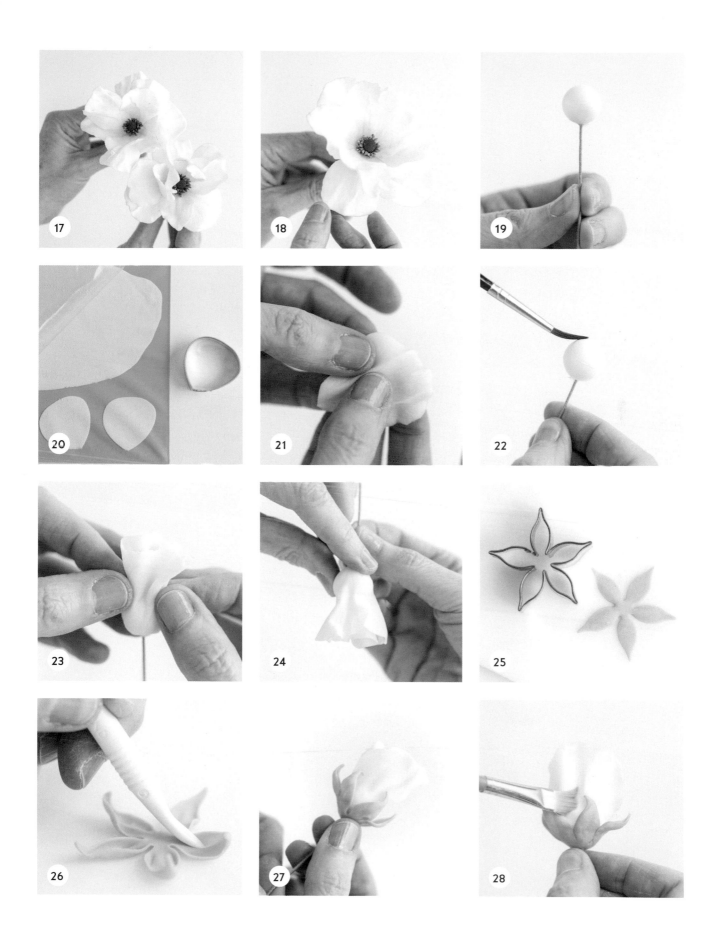

Forget-me-not

Cute and diminutive, forget-me-not flowers are a lasting symbol of remembrance. A myth describes a man swept away in a river after retrieving the beautiful blue blossoms for his true love, telling her not to forget him as he's floating away. They are tiny, delicate, and quick to make, and a wonderful choice for a filler flower if you need a spot of blue or purple in an arrangement. Additional varieties include pink and white, but the classic blue is my favorite.

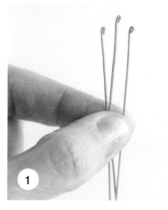

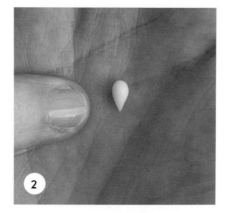

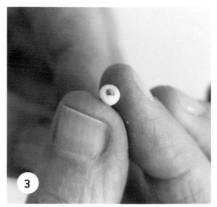

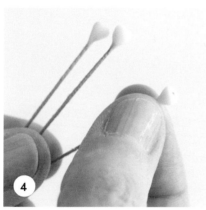

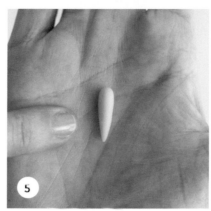

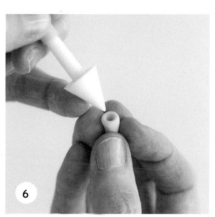

SPECIFICS YOU WILL NEED

···

- Yellow paste (Americolor Gel Lemon Yellow)
- Blue and/or purple paste (Americolor Gel Sky Blue, Royal Blue, Violet)
- Moss green paste (Wilton Moss Green)
- Calyx cutter: ⅝in (1.5cm) 6-petal cutter N7 (Orchard Products)
- 28g and 30g green wire
- Cone tool
- Royal Blue, Lavender and Kiwi petal dusts
- White edible paint (Wilton) (optional)

MAKE THE FLOWER CENTERS

1. Prepare 28g green wires by creating a tiny closed hook with pliers.

2. Roll a tiny ⅛in (3mm) ball of yellow paste into a teardrop shape.

3. Dab the hook with a tiny bit of sugar glue and insert the wire down through the top of the teardrop. Slide the paste up around the hook so just the tip is visible.

4. Gently press the paste to attach it to the wire. Leave it to dry.

MAKE THE FLOWERS

5. Roll a ¼in (5mm) ball of blue or blue/purple paste into a narrow ¾in (2cm) cone.

6. Press into the top of the cone with the cone tool, making an ⅛in (3mm) deep opening.

101

7. Use small scissors to snip five petals.

8. Open the petals with your fingertips and flatten each petal firmly between your thumb and finger.

9. Turn the blossom upside down on a foam pad. Using a ball tool, gently flatten and then stretch the petals a little bit.

10. Press the cone tool in the center of the flower to open it again.

11. Apply a tiny amount of glue to the yellow center.

12. Slide the wire down through the center of the blue blossom, stopping when yellow ring of paste around the hook is sitting at the top of the opening.

13. Secure the base of the blossom to the wire and leave to dry.

FINISH THE FLOWERS

14. Use a small paintbrush to edge the blossoms with a mixture of Royal Blue and Lavender petal dusts to define the petals. Steam to set the dust colors and leave the flowers to dry before using.

15. If desired, use a small detail brush and paint a tiny white line on or between each petal with white edible paint. This makes the blossoms more botanically correct, but I don't think it is necessary for the flower to be recognized.

MAKE THE BUDS

16. Roll ¼in (5mm) ball of blue or blue/purple paste and attach it to 30g hooked wire. Using a knife tool, make five equally spaced indentations around the bud.

17. Roll moss green paste thinly and cut a ⅝in (1.5cm) calyx shape. Cup the sections with a Dresden tool and attach to the base of the bud with glue. Leave to dry.

18. Dust the tip of the bud with a mixture of Royal Blue and Lavender petal dusts. Dust the calyx with Kiwi petal dust. Steam to set the dust colors and allow the buds to dry before using.

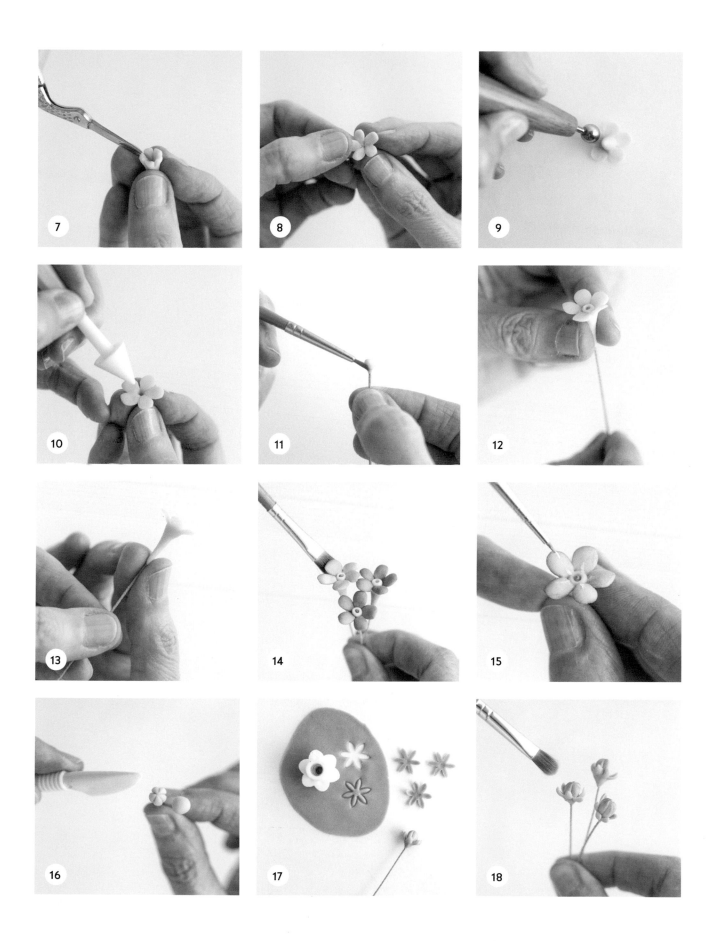

Petunia

These cheery garden favorites are available in an amazing range of colors and sizes and bloom from early summer until the first frost in the fall. The smaller blossoms are a lovely new filler flower to consider, while a larger version is big enough to stand in as a secondary flower to support focal flowers in your design. I've kept to soft pastels here, but don't be afraid to try some deeper hues for a late summer pop of color.

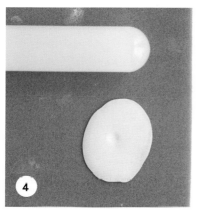

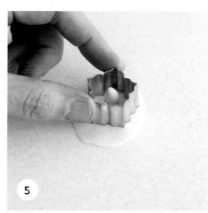

SPECIFICS YOU WILL NEED

···

- Pale pink paste (Wilton Pink)
- Yellow-green paste (Americolor Gel Avocado + Lemon Yellow)
- Petunia cutter, 1in (2.5cm) (World of Sugar Art)
- ⅞in (2.3cm) calyx cutter (PME brand)
- JEM veining tool
- 24g white wire
- Foam pad with ¼in (5mm) hole
- Needle tool
- Dresden tool
- Cone tool
- Magenta and Kiwi petal dusts

MAKE THE FLOWER

1. Prepare a 24g white wire by bending a ½in (1cm) long hook in it.

2. Roll a ⅝in (1.5cm) ball of pale pink paste into a teardrop shape.

3. Place the tip in a ¼in (5mm) hole in a foam pad.

4. Roll the protruding paste thinly with a rolling pin.

5. Remove the paste from the foam pad and cut a 1in (2.5cm) petunia petal shape.

6. With a ball tool on a foam pad, gently stretch the petals ¼in (5mm) with strokes from the center outwards.

7. Place the neck of the flower back in the ¼in (5mm) hole in the foam pad and vein each of the petals with the JEM veining tool.

8. With a needle tool, make a center vein on each petal by gently stroking from the outer tips towards the center. Keep the needle tool low and flat to prevent tearing the paste.

9. Take the flower out of the hole and flip it over. Ruffle the outer edges with a small ball tool.

10. Cup the underside of each petal with a Dresden tool or small ball tool, making two strokes on each petal on both sides of the center vein.

11. Dip a wire hook in sugar glue and insert it through the bottom end of the neck, sliding the hook halfway up. Gently roll the paste with your fingers to attach it to the wire and create a tapered end.

12. Press the flower center with the cone tool to make an indentation. Do not press deep enough to expose the wire hook.

13. Hang the flower to dry. Gently press the edges of the petals towards each other with your fingertips if you want a flower that is a bit more closed in appearance.

MAKE THE CALYX

14. Roll yellow-green paste thinly and cut a ⅞in (2.3cm) calyx shape. Thin the edges with a ball tool and cup each of the calyx sections with the Dresden tool.

15. Using a bit of sugar glue, attach the calyx with the sections curling up around the base of the flower.

DUST THE FINISHED FLOWER

16. Using a small paintbrush, dust the center of the flower with Magenta petal dust. Use a tiny detail brush to add the same color to the veins running down the middle of each petal.

17. Dust the calyx with Kiwi, extending the color onto the base of the flower. Steam to set the color and leave to dry before using.

18. If making a white petunia, dust Kiwi in the center and on the center veins to give it some life.

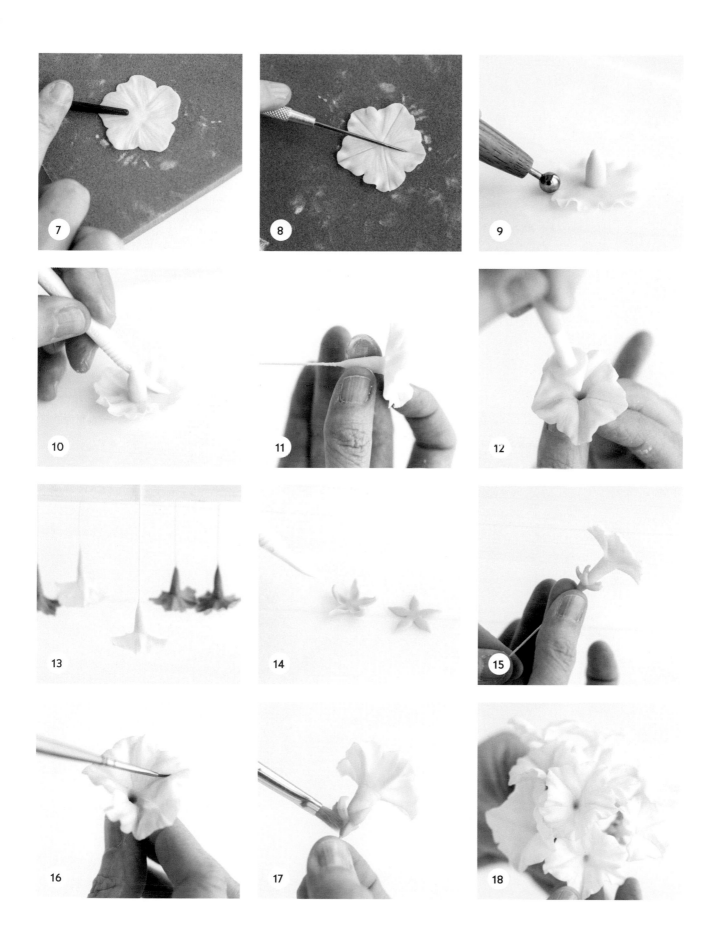

Clematis

Known as the "Queen of the Vine", there are over two hundred species of clematis, but I've presented a small four-petaled version here, perfect to use as a delicate filler flower. A spring bloomer, clematis come in a wide range of colors including purple, blue, pink, white and red. This one is quick to make with a thread center surrounded by wired petals. Make a few of the small leaves, add a flower or two, and you have a perfect trailing vine detail for your cake design.

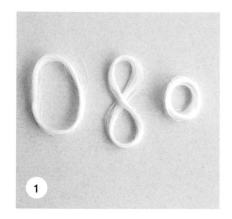

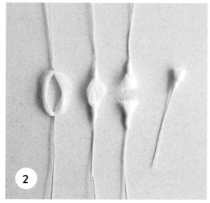

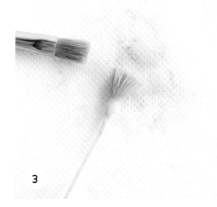

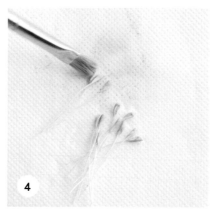

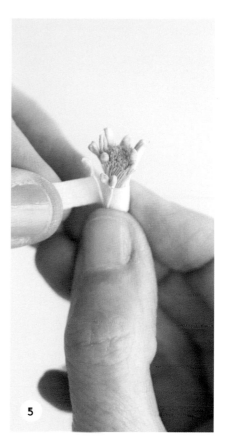

SPECIFICS YOU WILL NEED

....

- Purple (Wilton Violet + Pink), white and yellow-green paste (Americolor Gel Avocado + Lemon Yellow)
- Clematis petal and leaf cutter: ¾ x 1¾in (2 x 4.5cm) (Dahlia Petal cutters by World of Sugar Art)
- Clematis petal and leaf veiners (Marcel Veldbloem Flower Veiners)
- White sewing thread
- 30g white wire
- 28g and 30g green wire
- Acoustic "bumpy" foam
- Floral tape, white and green
- Stamens, long head, pointed or hammerhead
- Knife tool
- Kiwi, Lilac and Moss Green petal dusts

MAKE THE CENTER

1. Wrap white thread 50 times around three of your fingers to create a loop. Twist the loop into a figure-8 and then fold in half.

2. Insert a 6in (15cm) piece of 30g wire through middle of the loop and fold in half over one end. Twist the wire tightly at the base of the loop three times. Repeat with the opposite side. Wrap over the twisted wire and base of the thread tightly with half-width white floral tape. Repeat on the opposite end. Cut loop in half with sharp scissors. Trim each of the halves to ¼in (5mm) length with a flat top.

3. Dust the thread with Kiwi petal dust.

4. Dust 10–12 stamen heads with the same Kiwi petal dust.

5. Attach the stamens in several small groups with half-width white floral tape, wrapping tightly so the tips of the stamens are level with or just slightly above the top of the thread. Trim off some length of the stamen filaments to reduce the bulkiness in the final stem.

MAKE THE PETALS

6. Roll purple paste thinly on a groove board and cut a ¾ x 1¾in (2 x 4.5cm) petal shape.

7. Dip a 30g white wire tip in sugar glue and insert it ½in (1cm) into the groove. Secure at the base.

8. On a foam pad, lengthen the petal by ¼in (5mm) and widen it a bit with a ball tool.

9. Place the petal groove-side down in the veiner and then press it gently and evenly.

10. Remove the petal from the veiner and gently pinch the petal tip with your fingers if desired.

11. Lay the petal on "bumpy" foam to dry. Make four petals per flower.

DUST THE PETALS

12. Dust around the petal edges with Lilac dust. Add a bit more color at the base of the petal near the wire.

13. Add a tiny touch of Kiwi dust at the base of the petals.

ASSEMBLE THE FLOWER

14. Using half-width green floral tape, attach the first petal with its base lined up at the base of the thread center.

15. Add a second petal opposite the first one.

16. Add the remaining two petals spaced around the center so they create more of an X-shape versus an even cross shape. Steam to set the color and leave to dry before using.

17. Clematis flowers can be beautiful small fillers in white and pale pink.

MAKE THE CLEMATIS BUD

18. Roll a ½in (1cm) ball of white paste into a narrow cone ¾in (2cm) long and attach it to a hooked 28g green wire.

19. With a knife tool, mark four indentations from base to tip, evenly spaced around the cone. Leave the bud to dry.

20. Dust the color of the flower (Lilac is pictured) from above at the tip of the bud, and soft Kiwi at the base. Steam to set the colors and leave to dry before using.

MAKE THE CLEMATIS LEAVES

21. Roll yellow-green paste thinly over the groove board and cut a ¾ x 1¾in (2 x 4.5cm) leaf shape. Use the same cutter as for the clematis petals, but with the pointed tip at the top.

22. Dip the end of a 30g green wire in sugar glue and insert it ½in (1cm) into the groove.

23. With a ball tool, thin the edges of the leaf on the foam pad and then press it in the veiner.

24. Lay the leaf on foam to dry.

25. Dust with a mix of three parts Kiwi and one part Moss Green petal dusts. Steam to set the dust colors and leave to dry before using.

MAKE THE CLEMATIS VINE

26. Roll and tightly twist the top several inches of a piece of half-width green floral tape between your fingers to create a skinny tendril.

27. Attach the tail of the tendril to a 28g green wire and continue taping down the wire adding a few small leaves opposite each other or spaced unevenly along the stem.

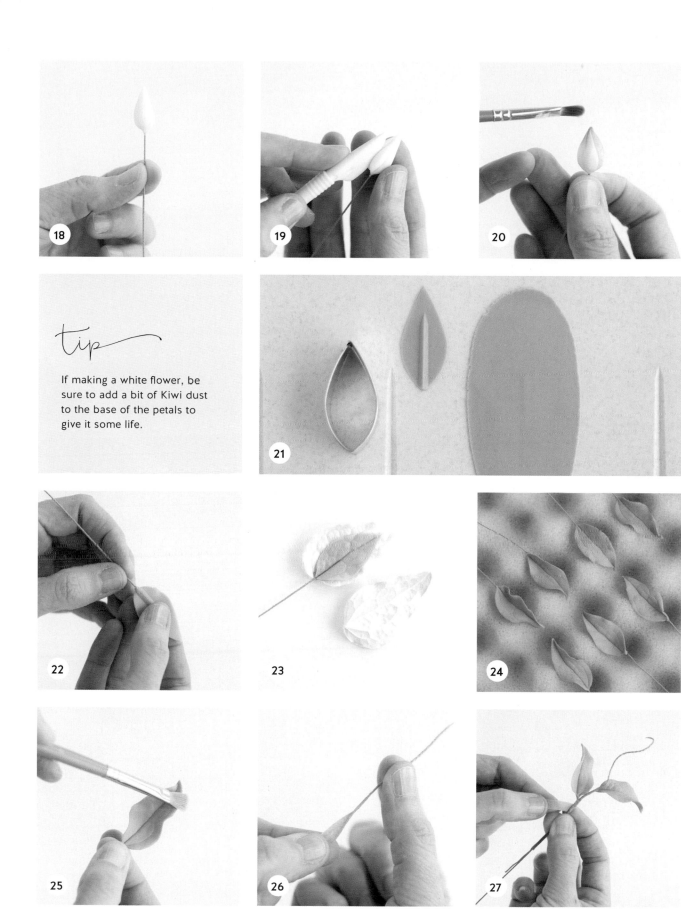

tip

If making a white flower, be sure to add a bit of Kiwi dust to the base of the petals to give it some life.

113

THE *Cake* PROJECTS

FOUNDATION LESSONS IN SUGAR FLOWER ARRANGING

There are a few different solutions for placing sugar flowers in cakes but be sure to also consult the guidelines of your local industry regulations and laws.

Tools and supplies you may need include floral tape, toothpicks, wooden skewers, straws or poly-dowels, small and large flower piks, wire cutters and pliers. You may also want to include gloves if desired.

Tape over the ends of all wires so they are not exposed **(1)**. Small flowers can be taped to toothpicks or cocktail sticks **(2),** and larger flowers can be taped to or created on wooden skewers **(3)**. The long skewer can be inserted farther into a cake, providing counter-balance for heavy or over-sized flowers. To use flower piks, straws or poly-dowels **(4)**, either position them in the cake before adding flower stems or secure the stems in the cavities before placing them in the cake. Use a small amount of fondant or royal icing to keep the stems in place.

COLOR HARMONY

This concept refers to aesthetically pleasing color combinations. Colors seen together that produce a positive response are said to be in harmony, and we can use these harmonies to achieve certain responses or moods. Pay attention to the color combinations that elicit positive feelings and reactions; these will be the ones you want to try in your designs. You can simply gather different mixes of sugar flowers in your hands to see if you like them together. Or you can research photos of real flower arrangements and pretty textiles as inspiration for color palettes and textures.

SHAPES

Consider both the shapes of the focal flowers on their own, and the shapes that are created between them when they are arranged together. Some flowers are cupped with a round base, others are v-shaped or flatter and more open. Some flowers will fit together closely, others will create gaps and openings that might need to be filled with smaller flowers or greenery. Practice arranging techniques on dummy cakes to train your eye to identify these shapes. This can also help avoid breakages as you won't be forcing flowers together.

FLOWER ARRANGING ORDER

1. Position and secure the focal and secondary flowers. Place a small ball of fondant in the space between them to insert the wires for the filler flowers and leaves. If desired, you can attach the fondant to the cake surface with a bit of water, sugar glue, royal icing or melted chocolate.

2. Fill the spaces between the flowers with greenery, other small blossoms, hydrangea, buds and single leaves, inserting the wires into the ball of fondant. If your greenery has weight you may need to secure it into the cake.

3. Begin filling any little gaps with filler flowers, small groups of berries or buds. Add more filler flowers or hydrangea in layers to add depth and texture to the arrangement.

SINGLE TIER
ARRANGEMENT WITH
Tulips

A beautiful single tier cake is the perfect way to celebrate anything! A birthday or anniversary, an engagement or intimate wedding, a new job or just because you are thinking about a loved one. Group your flowers offset near the edge of the cake, or spilling over that edge, and use a clean, simple finish on the cake to allow the sugar flowers to be the stars. Whether the design is lavish and elaborate or simple and minimalistic, both work really well here. Single tiers also offer a great opportunity to practice your arranging skills before working with a larger cake.

SPECIFICS YOU WILL NEED

....

CAKE TIER

- 5 x 6in (12.5 x 15cm) tier covered with white fondant

SPECIFIC SUPPLIES

- Additional white fondant
- 18in (46cm) yellow-green ¼in (5mm) wide grosgrain ribbon to finish the tier

FOCAL FLOWERS

- 2 single tulips, dark purple
- 1 double tulip, light purple

FILLER FLOWERS, BUDS AND LEAVES

- 10 green hydrangea flowers
- 3 purple hydrangea flowers
- 6 all-purpose buds
- 7 white filler flowers
- 3 mixed leaves
- 4 tulip leaves
- 2 greenery stems

1. Position and secure the tulips in an offset position on top of the cake.

2. Gently press a small amount of fondant to secure it on the cake between the bases of the tulips.

3. Position and insert the greenery and tulip leaves around the base of the tulips.

4. Begin filling the spaces between the tulips with hydrangea flowers and all-purpose buds. Fill any remaining little holes with the filler flowers.

AROUND A LEDGE
ARRANGEMENT WITH
Butterfly Ranunculus

The perfect solution for a cake displayed in the center of the party, this arrangement is designed to be beautiful from all angles! Highlight a mixed variety of flowers or share multiple colors of the same flower as shown here. Once you finish making your flowers, lay them out in a circle as a practice run so you can see how they will look all together. It's a great way to make sure the finished design will be fluid and balanced no matter which side your guests are viewing.

SPECIFICS YOU WILL NEED

CAKE TIERS

- 6 x 4in (15 x 10cm) tier covered with white fondant
- 8 x 6in (20 x 15cm) tier covered with ivory fondant

SPECIFIC SUPPLIES

- Additional ivory fondant
- 26in (65cm) soft beige/tan ⅜in (8mm) wide grosgrain ribbon to finish the bottom tier

FOCAL FLOWERS

- 8 butterfly ranunculus in a mix of yellow, white, ivory and pink
- 1 butterfly ranunculus bud
- 1 parrot tulip in soft peach
- 1 petunia in pink

FILLER FLOWERS, BUDS AND LEAVES

- Yellow berries
- Green berries
- 5 small dark green leaves
- 9 greenery stems with 3 leaves each
- 3 greenery stems with 5 leaves each

1. Prepare and stack the cake tiers. Finish the lower tier with ribbon. Lay out the large flowers and greenery in a circle to check the color pattern and positioning. You can use any ratio of butterfly ranunculus and parrot tulips that you wish. It's easier to make design changes at this step versus once you have the flowers on the cake.

2. Set aside one butterfly ranunculus for step 4. Position and secure the rest of the butterfly ranunculus, the parrot tulip, and the small leaves and greenery between the flowers, all on the ledge around the cake. Allow a small space offset to the front-right for the larger group of focal greenery. If desired, create a similar space on the rear of the cake.

3. Position and secure the focal greenery to fill the open space created in step 2. Layer the petunia over the pink butterfly ranunculus flower. Repeat on the rear of the cake if you are repeating the design.

4. Using the butterfly ranunculus set aside in step 2, position and secure the flower just below the ledge and nestled closely underneath the large group of focal greenery.

5. Insert the remaining leaves and stems at the base of the flowers so they hang below the arrangement.

6. Fill any gaps around the base of the parrot tulip with clusters of berries and a butterfly ranunculus bud. Turn the cake frequently as you work to check the arrangement and to make sure the design is complete from all directions.

tip

If you have a favorite type of flower, this design is a great way to show it off! Use the same flower in a variety of colors, or keep your palette monochromatic for a modern finish.

FRONT CASCADE ARRANGEMENT WITH

Poppies & Bougainvillea

A modern version of a floral cascade, the front arrangement is a voluminous visual masterpiece, drawing all of your attention to the full facing surface of a cake. Imagine stacked tiers with a bride's lavish bouquet nestled front and center, and overflowing toward the edges. Instead of placing sugar flowers in a cascading spiral, this lush arrangement is made up of focal flowers condensed in the middle section of the tiers, with outer edges that taper off using smaller blooms, delicate filler flowers and trailing greenery. And while this can be scaled for smaller cakes, a larger project will create a real "wow" moment.

SPECIFICS YOU WILL NEED

CAKE TIERS

- 4 x 6in (10 x 15cm) tier covered with white fondant
- 6 x 6in (15 x 15cm) tier covered with white fondant
- 8 x 5in (20 x 12.5cm) tier covered with white fondant

SPECIFIC SUPPLIES

- 62in (1.6m) yellow-green ¼in (5mm) wide grosgrain ribbon to finish the tiers

FOCAL FLOWERS

- 4 poppies
- 1 Japanese anemone
- 10 petunias
- 4 clematis
- 1 double tulip
- 25 clusters of bougainvillea (about 20 on stems and 5 clusters used as fillers)

FILLER FLOWERS, BUDS AND LEAVES

- 45 berries in 8 small clusters
- 10 hydrangeas
- 10 filler flowers
- 5 all-purpose buds
- 50 mixed small leaves (mostly taped in small branches of 5–7 leaves)

1. Prepare the cake tiers, stack and finish with ribbon. Position and secure the poppies and anemone across the front of the cake, a bit towards the right side (facing you). Begin with three poppies across the lower ledge of the cake and then layer the anemone and remaining poppy over the top edges of those flowers to make the focal flowers look full and lush.

2. Secure the lower bougainvillea branches in two areas on the cake, below the poppies to the left and right. Position the purple clematis next to the bougainvillea on the left.

3. Secure the upper bougainvillea branches above the left side of the poppies and going up to the top of the middle tier.

4. Mix in a few clematis flowers around the bougainvillea.

5. Position some of the greenery stems behind the bougainvillea and emerging from underneath the poppies.

6. Fill smaller gaps with petunias, clusters of berries, hydrangea and filler flowers.

7. Place the tulip on the lower left side and add greenery to fill out the design as desired.

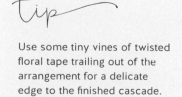

Use some tiny vines of twisted floral tape trailing out of the arrangement for a delicate edge to the finished cascade.

WREATH CAKE WITH

Heirloom Roses & Greenery

With so many gorgeous floral wreaths and garlands as inspiration, I hope you give this style of cake design a try! Whether it's delicate and sparse with a subtle hint of a wreath shape, or full and lush in a perfect oval or circle, any version is a stunning and unique way to decorate a cake. Build your wreath on the cake in stages so you can fine-tune the shape and make changes in your flowers and greenery as you go. Save the little fillers for the very end to hide wires and any gaps, and to build some beautiful depth.

SPECIFICS YOU WILL NEED

....

CAKE TIERS

- 6 x 6in (15 x 15cm) tier covered with white fondant
- 8 x 6in (20 x 15cm) tier covered with white fondant

SPECIFIC SUPPLIES

- 26in (65cm) yellow-green ¼in (5mm) wide grosgrain ribbon to finish the bottom tier
- Floral tape
- Toothpicks (cocktail sticks)

FOCAL FLOWERS

- 1 large heirloom rose
- 2 smaller heirloom roses (made with small petals only)
- 3 petunia blossoms
- 2 butterfly ranunculus flowers

FILLER FLOWERS, BUDS AND GREENERY

- 1 large straight branch, 15in (38cm), made with 3 smaller branches with 3 leaves each in the top half of the branch
- 1 curved branch 15in (38cm), made with 5 leaves spread out along the top half of the branch
- 1 small straight branch 7½in (19cm), made with 4 leaves
- Up to 5 single large leaves, same leaves as used on branches
- 1 curved branch, made with 2 branches of 3 leaves each, one 4in (10cm) and the other 6in (15cm)
- 2–3 small branches, 6–7in (15–18cm), made with 5 small leaves each
- 2 eucalyptus stems, 7in (18cm)
- 1 stem of brown leaves, 7in (18cm)

1. Prepare the cake tiers, stack them and finish the bottom tier with yellow-green ribbon. Prepare and tape the two main branches and the rest of the greenery as described in the Filler Flowers, Buds and Greenery list.

2. Insert and secure the two main branches (the straight one with nine leaves and the curved with five leaves) on the left side of the ledge. Tape a few single leaves to toothpicks and insert them over and between the branches to anchor the branches to the front of the cake tier.

3. Insert a third small branch with four leaves, which is as tall as the top tier, to fill out the vertical line of the greenery.

4. Position, secure and bend the two lower branches so they gently swoop across the front of the lower tier. The branches from steps 2–4 should begin to form a loose C-shape.

5. Add one stem each of greenery, brown leaves and eucalyptus to fill out the left vertical arrangement.

6. Position and secure two stems of leaves and a stem of eucalyptus on the cake ledge to create the right side vertical line of the "wreath" shape. Use a few more single leaves at the base of this grouping to hide the insertion point.

7. Position and secure the large heirloom rose on the ledge, over the insertion point of the left greenery arrangement.

8. Tuck the two smaller roses underneath the outer petals of the large rose so they stick out a bit.

9. Position and secure a butterfly ranunculus on the ledge just to the outside of the left side rose arrangement and the right side greenery grouping. These will give the wreath a bit more color and width, and help hide the insertion points.

10. Add the three petunias, one on the left above the large rose, and two on the right around the base of the greenery. Use additional flowers as desired to complete the arrangement.

LITTLE CAKES WITH
Mixed Flowers

Whether it is a romantic dessert for two, or an unforgettable sweet for one, little cakes are an extraordinary way to make someone feel special. It may be a bit of extra work to make the individual cakes, but it's so worth it when they can be decorated quickly and are so memorable. I've combined mixed flowers here but play with your favorite color palette or type of flower for a truly charming celebration!

SPECIFICS YOU WILL NEED

CAKES

- 2⅜in (6cm) sphere cakes covered with fondant
- 4 x 4in (10 x 10cm) cakes covered with fondant

SPECIFIC SUPPLIES

- Assorted ribbon
- Floral tape, white
- Toothpicks (cocktail sticks) or small flower piks

FLOWERS AND GREENERY

- Assorted single flowers including clematis, forget-me-nots, butterfly ranunculus, bougainvillea, gardenia, dogwood and Japanese anemone
- Greenery including single leaves and short branches of small leaves

1. Prepare your cakes and cover neatly with fondant. Finish the 4in (10cm) cakes with ribbon as desired.

2. Gather your flowers and greenery. Using white floral tape, group together single flowers and leaves, attaching the leaves directly under the base of the flower.

3. Tape the flower and leaves to a toothpick making sure to cover the ends of any wires. Or insert the stem into a small flower pik that has been filled with a bit of royal icing or melted white chocolate.

4. Insert the toothpick or flower pik into the cake. Gently arrange petals and leaves as desired to finish.

5. Arrange the cakes on a cake stand, serving dish or individual plates.

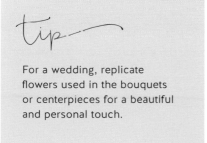

tip

For a wedding, replicate flowers used in the bouquets or centerpieces for a beautiful and personal touch.

MULTI-TIER ARRANGEMENT WITH
Poppies & Clematis

A favorite for larger weddings and celebrations, a multi-tiered cake is the perfect canvas for showcasing several beautiful sugar flower arrangements. While you want a well-balanced design, don't limit your creativity with a tried and true small upper arrangement and large lower arrangement. Extra fullness and a more luxurious look can be created easily with trailing flowers and greenery, resulting in arrangements that feel lush and modern.

SPECIFICS YOU WILL NEED

CAKE TIERS

- 4 x 6in (10 x 15cm) tier covered with white fondant
- 6 x 6in (15 x 15cm) tier covered with white fondant
- 8 x 5in (20 x 12.5cm) tier covered with white fondant

SPECIFIC SUPPLIES

- 66in (1.7m) yellow-green ¼in (5mm) wide grosgrain ribbon to finish the cake tiers
- Additional white fondant
- Floral tape

FOCAL FLOWERS

- 7 poppies (3 pale peach, 1 dark peach, 2 ivory, 1 white)
- 4 pink clematis flowers

FILLER FLOWERS, BUDS AND LEAVES

- 20 green hydrangea flowers
- 20 white filler flowers
- 12 all-purpose buds
- 3 large hydrangea leaves
- 2 vines with a tendril and 3–5 very small leaves
- 4 large greenery stems with 7 leaves each
- 4 small greenery stems with 3–4 small leaves each

1. Prepare the cake tiers, stack and finish with ribbon. Create the upper arrangement with three poppies between the top and middle tiers.

2. Create the lower arrangement with four poppies between the middle and bottom tiers.

3. Roll balls of fondant and secure these on the ledges between the poppies. Position and secure the large leaves at the outer edges of the arrangements. Position and secure the large greenery stems around the outer edges of the poppy arrangements. Insert the smaller greenery stems in a few of the gaps between the poppies. Mix one of the vine tendrils with the greenery stems on the lower arrangement.

4. Begin filling the remaining spaces between the poppies with hydrangea, buds and filler flowers.

5. Use floral tape to attach one of the tendril vines to one of the clematis flowers. Layer two of the clematis flowers over the top edges of the poppies to fill any remaining gaps in the upper arrangement.

6. Use your fingers to shape the tendril to fall away from the cake.

7. Position and secure the remaining two clematis flowers in the lower arrangement.

tip

Don't be afraid to layer your filler flowers to fill gaps. Start with a first layer to fill an opening, and then insert more over the top for a full, lush look.

SUPPLIERS

USA

WORLD OF SUGAR ART
www.worldofsugarart.com
Cutters, single-sided veiners, stamens,
sugarcraft tools and supplies

CK PRODUCTS
www.ckproducts.com
Essential and specialty supplies, CelBuds,
petal dust, plastic half sphere formers

CRYSTAL COLORS
www.sugarpaste.com
Petal dust (Kiwi, Moss Green, Holly,
Peach, Cream)

FIRST IMPRESSIONS MOLDS
www.firstimpressionsmolds.com
Silicone leaf and petal veiners

GLOBAL SUGAR ART
www.globalsugarart.com
Extensive range of tools and supplies,
masonite cake boards, cutters, veiners,
confectioner's glaze, gel colors, petal dust

**INTERNATIONAL SUGAR ART
COLLECTION**
www.nicholaslodge.com
Flower and leaf cutters, veiners, sugarcraft
tools and supplies, tylose, leaf glaze

MICHAEL'S CRAFT STORES
www.michaels.com
Aerated styrofoam balls, dusting brushes,
Celebrate It brand ribbon (yellow-green,
chocolate grosgrain and white)

PASTRY CHEF CENTRAL
www.pastrychef.com
Plastic half sphere molds

SMOOTHFOAM
www.smoothfoam.com
High-density styrofoam balls

SUGAR DELITES
www.sugardelites.com
Cutters, veiners, confectioner's glaze, floral
wire/tape, sugarcraft tools, gel colors

SUNFLOWER SUGAR ART
www.sunflowersugarartusa.com
Cutters, veiners, silicone molds

SUGAR ART STUDIO
www.sugarartstudio.com
Cutters, veiners, silicone molds

UK/EUROPE

SQUIRES KITCHEN SHOP
www.squires-shop.com
Cutters, Orchard Products cutters, Great
Impressions veiners, gel colors, petal dust,
leaf glaze, essential tools, stamens, flower piks

A PIECE OF CAKE
www.sugaricing.com
Essential and specialty tools and supplies

MARCEL VELDBLOEM FLOWER VEINERS
www.flowerveiners.nl
Rose petal veiners, flower and leaf veiners

CANADA

FLOUR CONFECTIONS
www.flourconfections.com
Extensive range of tools and supplies, half
sphere/petal formers, drying foam, stamens,
cutters, petal dust

THANK YOU

Thank you again to my wonderful team
at F&W Media! To Ame, Anna, Jane
and Jeni, thank you for the opportunity
to share more Petalsweet sugar flowers,
and for all your hard work in making
Volume 2 another special project.

I'm so grateful to work again with
the amazing team at Harper Point
Photography! Thank you, Nate and
Kira, for making all the photoshoots as
fun as they could be, and for making
sure every beautiful photo was pure
Petalsweet.

Thank you so much to my lovely
students for choosing to spend your
precious time in a workshop or class
with me. Your excitement learning
sugar flowers brings me great joy, and
I adore watching you fall in love with
the process! I'm so grateful to have the
opportunity to work with you.

So much love to my family and friends
for all your support! To my amazing
mom and step-dad, thank you for your
love and encouragement.

Finally, I'm so grateful to my wonderful
husband Keith. Thank you for always
being my number one fan. I love you
very much!

ABOUT THE AUTHOR

Owner, artist and Creative Director at Petalsweet, based in San Diego,
California, Jacqueline is a wedding cake artist turned sugarcraft and
cake decorating instructor. After falling in love with sugar flowers as a
hobby, Jacqueline studied with some of the best sugar flower makers
in the business, and soon after began her journey in cake. Officially
founded in 2005, Petalsweet cakes are known
for their clean and modern designs, decorated
with delicate, stylized sugar flowers in soft
pastel color palettes. Thrilled to share her love
for the art form, Jacqueline dedicates most
of her time to teaching her signature style of
cake decorating and sugar flowers, traveling
throughout the USA and internationally.

www.petalsweet.com

INDEX

A DAVID AND CHARLES BOOK
© David and Charles, Ltd 2019

David and Charles is an imprint of David and Charles, Ltd
1 Emperor Way, Exeter Business Park, Exeter, EX1 3QS

Text and Designs © Jacqueline Butler 2019
Layout and Photography © David and Charles, Ltd 2019

First published in the UK and USA in 2019

Jacqueline Butler has asserted her right to be identified as author of this work
in accordance with the Copyright, Designs and Patents Act, 1988.

A catalogue record for this book is available from the British Library.

ISBN-13: 978-1-4463-0729-8 hardback

ISBN-13: 978-1-4463-7735-2 EPUB

Printed in China by Hong Kong Graphics for:
David and Charles, Ltd
1 Emperor Way, Exeter Business Park, Exeter, EX1 3QS

10 9 8 7 6 5 4 3 2 1

Publishing Director: Ame Verso
Managing Editor: Jeni Hennah
Project Editor: Jane Trollope
Proofreader: Cheryl Brown
Design Manager: Anna Wade
Designer: Anna Wade and Emma Teagle
Photography: Nathan Rega
Production Manager: Beverley Richardson

David and Charles publishes high quality books on a wide range of subjects.

Layout of the digital edition of this book may vary depending on reader hardware
and display settings.